SEXUALITY
—— AND THE ——
BLACK CHURCH

SEXUALITY
—— AND THE ——
BLACK CHURCH

A Womanist Perspective

Kelly Brown Douglas

ORBIS BOOKS

Maryknoll, New York 10545

The Catholic Foreign Mission Society of America (Maryknoll) recruits and trains people for overseas missionary service. Through Orbis Books, Maryknoll aims to foster the international dialogue that is essential to mission. The books published, however, reflect the opinions of their authors and are not meant to represent the official position of the society.

Queries regarding rights and permissions should be addressed to: Orbis Books, P.O. Box 308, Maryknoll, New York 10545-0308.

Published by Orbis Books, Maryknoll, NY 10545-0308
Manufactured in the United States of America

Scripture quotations are from the New Revised Standard Version, copyright © 1989 by the Division of Christian Education of the National Council of the Churches of Christ in the United States of America.

Library of Congress Cataloging-in-Publication Data
Douglas, Kelly Brown.
    Sexuality and the Black church : a womanist perspective / Kelly Brown Douglas.
        p.   cm.
    Includes bibliographical references and index.
    ISBN 1-57075-242-7 (pbk.)
    1. Womanist theology.   2. Sex – Religious aspects – Christianity.
    3. Afro-Americans – Sexual behavior.   I. Title.
    BT83.9.D68   1999
    230'.082 – dc21   98–32189

This is for you, Lloyd James Miller,
January 1955 – July 1994

Contents

Acknowledgments

Despite the many lonely hours I spent reading and writing in the darkness of the morning, this project could not have been done alone. There are many people, far too numerous to singularly mention, who did or said just the right thing, at just the right time, to encourage and support this work. To all of them, I am grateful. There are those, however, whose support of this part of my theological journey deserves public acknowledgment.

This project would never have been launched or completed without the support of Orbis Books. I thank especially Robert Ellsberg, who brought this book to the attention of Orbis and worked with me through the early outline and draft. I am also deeply appreciative of the many hours that Susan Perry put into this work, as she gave herself to the oftentimes tedious editorial work on the final draft.

In the loneliest of moments, when hurdles of research, writing, and time seemed almost insurmountable, there was a "great cloud of witnesses" whose presence became real in my life as they spurred me on toward completion. To Dickie, Bill, Rufus, Jim, William, and Wayland, I say thanks for keeping watch over me even as you have crossed on over before me.

Regardless of my commitment to this project, it could not have come to fruition without the resources of time and funding. I am especially thankful for the support of my colleagues at the Howard University School of Divinity, but specifically for the unqualified assistance of my deans, Clarence G. Newsome and Henry J. Ferry. Not only did they grant me the privilege of a sabbatical, and find money to support it, but they both gave of themselves to make sure that my sabbatical was productive. I am also extremely thankful for the support of the Episcopal Office of Black Ministries under the direction of Reverend Lynn Collins. When this project was only a proposal, Reverend Collins affirmed its benefit for the church and provided me with resources to make sure it happened and with opportunities to engage Episcopal church people on issues of sexuality. I am also very thankful for the enthusiastic support of my bishop, the bishop of southern Ohio, the

Right Reverend Herbert Thompson, who made it possible for me to receive a grant from the diocese's Professional Development Committee. I must also acknowledge the unflagging support of the bishop of Washington, D.C., the Right Reverend Ronald Haines. Through conversation, lunches, and the reading of my manuscript, as well as his prophetic witness in regard to gay and lesbian ordination, Bishop Haines has affirmed the importance of my work and encouraged the development of my ministry.

When you write alone, it is always nice to have a place to test your ideas and to receive critical feedback. I thank Pernessa Seele with Balm in Gilead Inc.; Reverend Ted Karpf, formerly with the National Episcopal AIDS Coalition; Reverend Carlton Veazey, with the Religious Coalition for Reproductive Choice; and Belva Boone with the Universal Fellowship of Metropolitan Community Churches — all of whom saw merit in my work long before others did and provided me with the forum to share my thoughts. I am also deeply appreciative of the students in my fall 1997 course, "Sexual Issues and the Black Church." Their weekly discussions only strengthened this book. I am particularly grateful to Beverly Goines, a student in that class, who worked without payment as a research assistant for this project. Thanks for helping me with everything from finding articles to using my computer.

One day history must tell the story of a group of womanist religious scholars who, though all scattered around the globe, traversed cyberspace and lived into the womanist idea by supporting one another in their movements toward "wholeness." To my womanist sisters I am so deeply indebted. Thank you for your prayers, your insights, your messages, your scholarly exchange and debate. When the night got long and I got weary, I knew that if I launched out into cyberspace I would find a word from one of you that would spur me on. I am especially thankful for my sister-friends Lisa Anderson, Renee Hill, Yvette Abraham, Cheryl Townsend Gilkes, Katie Cannon, Emilie Townes, Karen Baker-Fletcher, and Renita Weems. Thanks "y'all" for allowing me to pick your brains, take your time, and sometimes be a nuisance.

Truly no journey is walked alone. And while many have walked with me, there have been two who often see more in me than I do in myself, and who sometimes hear the call of my theological voice more clearly than I. James H. Cone and D. H. Kortright Davis mean more to me on my journey than any words could ever express. I simply thank them for their own profound theological witness and commitments to justice and for unconditionally being mentors and friends.

And without my loving family, nothing would be possible. I will always be grateful to my parents, William and Mary Brown, for their belief in me. I am most blessed by the love, support, and patience of my son and my husband. My son, Desmond, often laying on my office floor with pillow and covers, cajoled his mommy to finish her work so that I could play race cars with him. His mere loving presence reminded me of why what I try to do is important. And how do I say thanks to my husband, Lamont, who dared to marry a "theologian" and who every minute of the day makes my work possible as he affirms it and me?

Introduction

If someone had told me five years ago that I would be writing a book on Black sexuality, I would have replied, "You're crazy." At that time in my theological journey I simply had not given any thought to such a topic. But now, here I am writing this book, trying to untangle the complex reality of Black sexuality as well as to discern a theology in regard to the same. Sometimes a person chooses a subject, and other times a subject chooses a person. This issue of Black sexuality chose me. How did it happen? How did I get to this place?

My journey began with a trenchant critique by Renee Hill, one of my friends and theological colleagues. She stridently and rightly observed that her womanist theological colleagues had imprudently ignored the issue of sexuality. Hill wrote:

> Christian womanists have failed to recognize heterosexism and homophobia as points of oppression that need to be resisted if *all* Black women (straight, lesbian, and bisexual) are to have liberation and a sense of their own power. Some women have avoided the issue of sexuality and sexual orientation by being selective in appropriating parts of [Alice] Walker's definition of womanism. This tendency to be selective implies that it is possible to be selective about who deserves liberation and visibility.[1]

Though I had consistently argued that womanist theologians need to advocate against homophobia/heterosexism, Hill was right. At the time of her critique, neither I nor any other womanist religious scholar had given any sustained consideration to issues of homophobia/heterosexism or any other issue related to Black sexuality. What was going on? Why was even womanist theology — a theology recognized by some as providing one of the most holistic visions for human life and freedom — so silent on sexuality? Why were we womanist theologians, who so aptly criticize Black and feminist theologians for their failure to comprehend the complexity of Black women's oppression, so disinclined to confront the oppression of lesbians or broadly the presence of homophobia/heterosexism within the Black community? Alice Walker's definition,

1

which empowered us to speak as womanists, clearly affirmed the importance of human sexuality. Why were we so easily able to ignore, if not to
dismiss categorically, this aspect of her definition?[2] Why were our voices
so quiet, virtually mute, when it came to matters of sexuality? These
were questions which troubled me long after Hill's challenging indict-
ment. These concerns became even more pressing for me as events in
my personal life unfolded.

Over the last several years I have lost numerous close friends to
complications from HIV/AIDS. I ministered to and/or officiated at the
funerals for many of these persons. No loss had any greater impact upon
my life and theology than that of my oldest and closest friend, whom I
called Cousin Lloyd.

Lloyd and I grew up together in Dayton, Ohio. We traveled the same
social circles of Jack and Jill, Tots 'n Teens, swimming parties, and other
such activities of the Black middle class. In our growing up I was always
drawn to Lloyd on the many occasions we were together, because he
was frequently the object of teasing since he was not like the other
boys. In the words of our young playmates, Lloyd was a "sissy." In actual
fact, Lloyd simply had different interests than many of the other boys.
He preferred fashion, tennis, and academics to football, basketball, or
baseball. I empathized with Lloyd from afar, because I too was often the
source of ridicule, even by those closest to me. I preferred sports over
dolls, jeans over dresses, reading over play. So while Lloyd was called
a sissy, I was called a tomboy, all because of how we dared to defy the
standards of what it meant to be a boy or a girl.

As time went on, Lloyd and I would both end up in New York,
where we shared an apartment for two years during my doctoral studies
at Union Theological Seminary. During that time in New York, Lloyd
and I reflected on the pains and joys of our growing up, of our life.
We celebrated and cherished our friendship together and affirmed each
other's worth as human beings. More particularly, it was through my
relationship with Lloyd that I really began to recognize the alienation
experienced by Black people living with HIV/AIDS, particularly gay
persons, in relation to the Black church and wider Black community.

Black churches have gained a well-deserved reputation for being
slow in constructively responding to the AIDS crisis. Though AIDS
is devastating the Black community, Black churches have been reti-
cent to become involved in HIV/AIDS education and outreach. While
African Americans make up 13 percent of the U.S. population, they account for about 57 percent of all new HIV/AIDS infections. Moreover,

while the death rate from AIDS is decreasing in the overall population, AIDS remains the leading cause of death among Black people ages twenty-five to forty-four. Yet, despite evidence that suggests otherwise (for instance, among Black women, who make up 56 percent of the total AIDS cases among females, heterosexual sex is the most common route to infection), far too many in the Black church community continue to consider AIDS a "gay" disease. Reverend Kwabena Rainey Cheeks, a pastor who has been HIV positive for fourteen years, says, "When you deal with AIDS you have to deal with all of the issues, all of the isms of [the Black] community.... You can't touch AIDS and not deal with homophobia."[3] Surgeon General David Satcher echoes these sentiments when he says, "I grew up in the black church.... I think the church has problems with the life style of homosexuality."[4] The inappropriate association between HIV/AIDS and homosexuality has been perhaps the critical factor in causing Black passivity in regard to the AIDS crisis. This crisis has stridently brought to the surface the homophobia present within the Black church and community.

Many Black church people have unabashedly proclaimed that "they" (that is, homosexuals) have no business engaging in the sinful behaviors that lead to AIDS. Some Black preachers have admonished their congregations that homosexuality is a sin, and though we are to love the sinner, we must hate the sin. Others have called homosexuality nothing less than an "abomination."

Because Lloyd was quite simply one of the best human beings I have ever had the pleasure of knowing, I can no longer sit quietly by and let him be ridiculed or castigated. I can no longer use childhood as an excuse for being silent when others slur his name by association, and impugn his worth as a human being. I cannot be a silent bystander and permit Black church people to condemn him and other gay and lesbian persons, consigning them to death by way of AIDS. That I had to break my theological silence on this matter became even clearer to me during a public presentation.

One day in the middle of a lecture when I was addressing homophobia in a relatively "safe" manner by making parallels between it and racism, I was struck by something deep within me that said I had to say more than that. For the sake of Lloyd, and others like him, I had to broaden my theological discussion. I was urged to move beyond the glib responses to homophobia/heterosexism and to discern the complexity of its existence in the Black community. I was compelled toward a deeper discussion of Black sexuality. I knew that somehow if I was going to make any kind of difference in combating homophobia in the Black community, I had to understand the intricacies of what made the issue so potent and intractable. I had to know more about Black sexuality. It was then that I felt the call of God. What, I wondered, might the God of Jesus Christ be saying to me, a Black female, a womanist theologian, and the rest of the Black community about matters of sexuality, especially that of Black women and men? It is with these concerns that I have come to this particular theological discourse. It is a discussion that began with a theological challenge from a colleague and became more urgent as the result of a personal journey with my friend and cousin.

Since I resolved to begin this exploration, and since Hill's challenge, other womanist religious scholars have affirmed the importance of breaking the silence about Black sexuality. Particularly driven by the destruction the Black community has suffered as a result of HIV/AIDS, some womanist scholars are calling for serious theological and ethical reflection on issues of homophobia and heterosexism. No one has done this more consistently than ethicist Toinette Eugene. Pointing to the way in which HIV/AIDS destroys Black family systems, Eugene challenges the Black church, especially the Black Catholic church, of which she is a part, to become more responsive to the HIV/AIDS epidemic in the Black community. While she recognizes the Black churches' reticence to deal with this disease because of its association with homosexuals, she challenges the Black churches "not to forget" their historic role in nurturing life and freedom for Black men and women. Eugene implores the Black church to remember its prophetic past and, "[a]s a remembering, reconciling, and caring institution and a symbolic extended family, ... [to] be with its most vulnerable members as they die from or suffer and live with AIDS."[5]

Womanist ethicist Emilie Townes has also been vocal about the need to address matters of sexuality. Similarly fueled by the potential for HIV/AIDS to virtually destroy Black families and communities, Townes urges the Black community to break the death-dealing cycle of "sexual repression" — that is, being sexually active yet refusing to speak about sexual matters. She says such sexual repression is indeed killing the community as it allows for misunderstanding the relationship between HIV/AIDS and homosexuality. Again, she asserts that as long as this link remains so strong in a community (the Black community) where homophobia is so potent, HIV/AIDS will continue to grow unabated. Townes also recognizes in her discussion the relationship between the prevalence of sexism and "sexual repression."[6]

Karen Baker-Fletcher, in dialogue with Garth Kasimu Baker-Fletcher, likewise concedes that it is essential for the Black church to confront the potentially divisive issue of homosexuality. Yet she also admits that womanist theologians have been reluctant to do so. She says, "I sometimes wonder why womanists, myself included, are not more forthright about this particular subject. I suspect that for many it is for the same reason that many gays and lesbians hesitate to come out of the closet: fear of losing a job, of being thrown out of church, ostracized in community."[7]

This particular project attempts to heed the challenge of HIV/AIDS, homophobia/heterosexism, and most significantly the womanist task to foster the "survival and wholeness" of all people by shattering the silence concerning Black sexuality in general. As I began this project I quickly discovered that the passion surrounding homosexuality in the Black church and community is not simply a matter of sexual bigotry. Rather, the issue is much more complex. Homophobia is but one of the symptoms of a problematic understanding of sexuality present within the Black community. So again, while this journey began with a concern about homophobia, that is not the singular focus of this book. This book is an attempt to probe the conundrum of Black sexuality, especially as it relates to Black theological silence about sexuality.

If who we are — that is, our life experiences — helps us to determine our theological questions and concerns, then who we are also circumscribes those questions and concerns. Our particular social, historical, cultural, and political actualities can free us to address certain topics, and at other times those very same actualities can hinder us from doing so. Likewise, these life circumstances can assist us in perceiving the meaning of God's revelation, or they can obstruct our view of that revelation.

God's revelation does have meaning and significance in relation to issues of sexuality as they affect the Black church and community. Yet our history of oppression as Blacks in America has impeded the Black church and community from appropriating the meaning of God's revelation on this matter, and it has also contributed to a slow response to HIV/AIDS — even as it has contributed to a void in womanist theological discourse when it comes to the complexity of Black sexuality.

This book represents my efforts to fill that void. Its purpose is threefold: (1) to understand why sexuality in general has been a "taboo" subject for the Black church and community; (2) to advance womanist discourse on Black sexuality; and (3) to promote the kind of theological discourse and analyses that might nurture healthier attitudes and behaviors toward sexually related concerns within the Black church and community, especially concerns about homophobia/heterosexism.

In carrying forth this threefold purpose, my approach reflects my own theological journey. I will not begin with theological answers concerning what ought to be said about Black sexuality; instead, I will begin where most theological discussions begin — with questions. This means that this book begins not with formal "God-talk," but with the reality out of which God-talk, especially womanist God-talk, emerges. It starts by trying to understand the social-historical context that has shaped Black people's response to sexuality.

Fundamental to appreciating the arguments about Black sexuality made throughout this text is an accurate and comprehensive definition of sexuality. Christian ethicist James Nelson provides a definition that will be operative throughout this book. He accurately clarifies that sexuality is about more than what we do with our genitals. Sexuality is not synonymous with sex. Rather, while sexuality is not the whole of who we are as human beings, it is basic to who we are. It compels our emotional, affective, sensual, and spiritual relationships. Sexuality does not determine all our feelings, thoughts, and interactions, but it certainly permeates and affects them. Sexuality involves our self-understanding and our way of relating in the world as women and men. Nelson captures sexuality best when he says:

> Sexuality is a sign, a symbol, and a means of our call to communication and communion. This is the most apparent in regard to other human beings, and other body-selves. The mystery of our sexuality is the mystery of our need to reach out to embrace others both physically and spiritually.... [Sexuality] is who we *are* as body-selves who experience the emotional, cognitive, physical, and spiritual need for intimate communion — human and divine.[8]

Readers should keep in mind this comprehensive understanding of human sexuality as they move through this text. Let us now look specifically at how we shall proceed.

Part 1: The Roots of Black Theological Silence

Part 1 seeks to determine why Black churches and the Black theological community in particular have been so reluctant to discuss matters of sexuality. This section argues that White racist culture has significantly contributed to Black people's attitudes toward sexuality, especially toward their own sexuality. Chapter 1 carefully examines the essential function of Black sexuality in White culture. It argues that the exploitation and manipulation of Black sexuality are crucial to the maintenance of White patriarchal hegemony in America. Michel Foucault's theory of power is utilized to support this argument.

Chapter 2 looks specifically at the way Black sexuality has been impugned by White culture. It examines the various sexual myths, stereotypes, and concomitant laws and customs directed toward Black people's sexuality. An understanding of these particular assaults helps one to appreciate the complexity of Black silence in regard to sexual issues.

Part 2: The Impact of the White Cultural Attack

Part 2 examines Black people's responses to the White cultural assault upon their sexuality. The underlying assumption of this chapter is that this assault has rendered sexuality virtually a taboo issue in the Black community. In other words, the Black church and community have been reluctant to engage in frank and comprehensive sexual discourse because of the way Blacks' sexuality has been exploited. Chapter 3 makes this argument directly and also explores the ramifications of Black people maintaining silence about sexual issues. Chapter 4 specifically addresses homophobia/heterosexism in the Black church and community. It attempts to understand the intransigence of Black homophobia/heterosexism in light of Black sexual oppression. In this chapter homophobia refers to the oppressive and bigoted attitudes and behaviors that Black people, as well as others, often direct toward gay and lesbian persons. Heterosexism signals the complex systems and structures that privilege heterosexual orientations, while explicitly or implicitly penalizing same-sexed orientations. Both chapters 3 and 4 suggest the need for a Black sexual discourse of resistance.

Part 3: A Theology of Black Sexuality

Part 3 examines the responses of the Black church and Black theology to Black sexuality. Chapter 5 specifically addresses the mandate of Black Christians to engage in sexual discourse. It clarifies the inextricable connection between the God of Jesus Christ and human sexuality. It specifically looks at this in terms of the Black faith tradition and clarifies the special womanist mandate to advance a sexual discourse of resistance. Chapter 6 suggests ways in which sexual discourse can be nurtured in the Black church and community as well as the implications for Black church actions in regard to sexual issues.

This book does not intend to provide all of the theological answers, or even to raise all of the right questions, in relation to the complex concerns surrounding Black sexuality. I only hope through this work to provoke the kind of sustained analysis, discourse, attitudes, and behaviors that will move *all* Black women and men closer to enjoying the fullness and uniqueness of their humanity. If, indeed, womanist theology is accountable to "ordinary" Black people as they struggle through life to "make do and do better," then as a womanist theologian I am compelled to do my best, despite my limitations, to contribute as boldly as I can to the Black struggle for life and wholeness. And so I offer this book.

PART 1

THE ROOTS OF BLACK THEOLOGICAL SILENCE

CHAPTER 1

Black Sexuality

A Pawn of White Culture

Growing up Black in America means discovering early in life the various stereotypes that surround blackness. Many of these stereotypes involve sexuality. Whether one learns through the oral tradition of Black popular culture or the tragedies of Black history, an early lesson of Black youth is that White culture regards Black men and women as highly sexualized, lascivious beings. To hear a White person remark, whether in earnest or jest, about Black men's sexual prowess or Black women's sexual promiscuity is not an uncommon experience for most Black people. But why is this the case? Why is Black sexuality so vulnerable to ridicule and exploitation in American society? Why is an attack upon Black sexuality so crucial to White culture?

A popular belief among Black people is that White America's preoccupation with Black sexuality reflects White people's fascination with, yet fear of, the same. There is little doubt that a White pathology of fascination and fear in regard to Black sexuality does exist. Recent historical events strongly attest to this. One such historical indicator was the unnecessary public spectacle that the U.S. Congress and the mass media made of Anita Hill and Clarence Thomas during Thomas's confirmation hearings on his nomination to the Supreme Court.[1] With the hearings broadcast from gavel to gavel on every major television network, White Americans were able to peer into certain sexual behaviors of two Black people. As male White senators "dutifully" extracted from Hill vulgar details of Thomas's alleged sexual harassment, many White Americans undoubtedly confirmed their deep-seated fears concerning Black people's sexual deviance, while also satisfying their fascination with Black people's sexual activity. As bell hooks aptly observed, "[U]ltimately the Thomas hearings were not

11

only a public political spectacle orchestrated by whites but...whites were, indeed, the intended audience. The rest of us were merely voyeurs."[2]

The circuslike attraction to the 1995–96 criminal trial and subsequent 1996–97 civil trial of O. J. Simpson further evinces the prevalence of White fascination and fear about Black sexuality. For many White Americans, Simpson's guilt or innocence was less a factor than making clear that he, as a Black man, would have to pay the price for what they perceived as his flamboyant sexual involvement with a "model" White woman (namely, blonde and blue-eyed). In any case, he would have to pay the price for allegedly abusing and killing her. The specter of race and sex pervaded the entire internationally broadcast Simpson fiasco.[3]

Yet, as obvious and real as White fascination and fear are in relation to Black sexuality, alone they do not explain this kind of sustained attention. These two factors do not adequately account for the consistent barrage of malicious and denigrating attacks made upon Black men's and women's sexuality throughout American history. Even when reflecting upon such an event as the Hill and Thomas exhibition, it soon becomes clear that something more was at stake for White America. bell hooks points to this when she says of that spectacle:

> We were witnessing yet another plantation drama where the labor and bodies of black folks were made to serve the interests of a system that has no intention of fostering and promoting the social and political growth of black people or eradicating racism and white supremacy.[4]

White America's fixation with Black sexuality appears to be grounded in something more integral to the very existence of White society. Indeed, the violation of Black sexuality by White culture is about nothing less than preserving White power in an interlocking system of racist, classist, sexist, and heterosexist oppression.

This chapter will show that the exploitation of Black sexuality is inevitable and, in fact, essential for White culture as it serves to nurture White patriarchal hegemony. First I will define the nature of White culture and then try to discern the significance of sexuality for it. As a theologian, I am paying special attention to the role of Christianity in shaping cultural responses to human sexuality. My primary framework for understanding the role of sexuality in society is Michel Foucault's theory of power. Because Foucault's analysis is unapologetically "Francocentric" and "Eurocentric," and thus virtually ignores matters of race, I intend to complement his inquiry with insights from Black female and male social critics. These insights should help answer the specific question, Why does White culture malign Black sexuality? and should help us begin to apprehend the complexity of Black people's attitudes toward sexual issues.

WHITE CULTURE

Attacks on Black sexuality seem intrinsic to White culture. A full appreciation of the intimate bond between Black sexuality and White culture necessitates a precise understanding of this culture. Literary genius and social critic James Baldwin helps to provide such an understanding. Attempting to determine the "price of the ticket" for being Black and male in America, Baldwin comments on the "price of the ticket" for being White in America:

> They come through Ellis Island where *Giorgio* becomes Joe, *Pappavasiliu* becomes Palmer, *Evangelos* becomes Evans, *Goldsmith* becomes Smith or Gold, and *Avakian* becomes King. So, with a painless change of name, and in the twinkling of an eye, one becomes a white American....
>
> The price the white American paid for his ticket was to become white —: and, in the main, nothing more than that, or, as he was to insist, nothing less.[5]

Baldwin gives a vivid description of a cultural phenomenon that occurred as Europeans invaded what for them was a "New World," America. Whether they came through Ellis Island or by an earlier, more dubious route, Europeans, reflecting the ethnic and cultural diversity of their continent, encroached upon America. They arrived as Irish, Italian, English, German, and various other ethnic and cultural groups from Europe. Yet somewhere on the shores of America they established a new identity. They became White. They subordinated their ethnic and cultural particularities in order to adopt a common national identity as *White* Americans.

The Meaning of Whiteness

At least two salient features have been used to determine whiteness in America: ethnic heritage and physical appearance. Initially, it seemed not to matter why one came to America or even what was one's economic or class status prior to coming. The "ticket" to whiteness was arrival from Europe. The varied ethnicities were supplanted by whiteness. The fact that there were few restrictions on intermarriage between the various European ethnic groups suggests the unimportance of maintaining a pure and complete ethnic identity in the "New World."

White identity was further based on physical appearance. The "normative classical gaze" that emerged during the Western Enlightenment was no doubt fundamental to a visual assessment of whiteness in the new world of America. According to Cornel West, this "gaze" was achieved during the Enlightenment recovery of "classical antiquity."[6] This recovery not only nurtured an admiration for Greek art and scholarship but also cultivated an awe for Greek beauty. Greek bodies and physical appearance were admired. The dominant Western culture held in high esteem those physical characteristics that most resembled those of the Greeks. Not surprisingly, European skin color and phenotype were deemed to approximate those of the Greeks — even though what was understood as typical European physiognomy (that is, blond hair and blue eyes) was atypical of Greek characteristics. Nevertheless, with the relationship drawn between Greeks' physiognomy and that of Europeans, it was easier to establish not only who was White but also the superiority of whiteness. West explains:

> What is distinctive about the role of the classical aesthetic and cultural norms at the advent of modernity is that they provided an acceptable authority for the idea of white supremacy, an acceptable authority that was closely linked with the major authority on truth and knowledge in the modern world, namely, the institution of science.[7]

The link between science and White supremacy, which West notes, was forged in eighteenth-century Europe as scientists and anthropologists began to conduct studies to discern the origin of skin color. This research was motivated in large measure by the appearance of the "Negro." Historian Winthrop Jordan notes the problematic when he suggests, "The question of the color of man was pre-eminently the question of the color of the 'Negro.'"[8] The concern was to establish that a skin color so diametrically opposed to whiteness was not in some regard "superior" to whiteness. As Jordan further points out, "It was not so much a matter of why the Negro was black as why the Negro had become the very negation of white."[9]

Though there were those who argued that White and Black people were of different species and shared no common ancestry, the dominant assumption of the eighteenth century was that the two races of people shared a common origin and thus were "members of the same species."[10] Underlying this "monogenesis" theory, however, was the widely held notion that the original color of humanity was White. Black skin color was viewed as a severe aberration of whiteness. Numerous studies on the origins of skin color confirmed this "scientific" myth. In his 1774 volume *History of the Earth*, Oliver Goldsmith suggested that variations of human color "are actual marks of the degeneracy in the human form; and we may consider the European figure and colour as standards to which to refer all other varieties, and with which to compare them."[11] As Jordan goes on to point out, "The concept of degeneration from primitive whiteness was seemingly confirmed by a curious phenomenon: Negro babies are born considerably lighter than they shortly become, a fact which many eighteenth-century writers noted with almost gleeful interest."[12]

While the "scholarship" of eighteenth-century Europe — which suggested the inherent inferiority of Black-skinned people — certainly laid a firm foundation for a comprehensive ideology of White supremacy, such an "intellectually" based ideology did not fully emerge in the United States until the nineteenth century. Following the lead of their European colleagues, American scholars explained blackness as a sign of degeneracy. Eminent physician and "humanitarian" Benjamin Rush speculated in a 1792 presentation to the American Philosophical Society that the "Negro's" color was due to leprosy. This disease, he concluded, could also explain "Negro features," meaning big lips and flat noses.[13] Still others suggested that the color difference had to do with climate. The influence of the Greek normative gaze was most evident in these climate-based explanations. Stanley Stanhope Smith, a prominent eighteenth-century educator and former president of Princeton University, put the matter plainly:

> It may perhaps gratify my countrymen to reflect that the United States occupy those latitudes that have ever been most favourable to the beauty of the human form. When time shall have accommodated the constitution of its new state, and cultivation shall have meliorated the climate, the beauties of Greece and Circassia may be renewed in America; as there are not a few already who rival those of any quarter of the globe.[14]

The rise in the United States of "intellectual" arguments that vindicated White supremacy by asserting Black inferiority coincided with the rise of the abolitionist movement. This movement forced slave apologists to articulate the "positive good" of enslavement, such as, slavery controls and perhaps civilizes otherwise savage beings. In this regard, the fact of a person's Black skin color was reason enough to enslave him or her. Slavery and blackness became virtually synonymous. A missionary for the Society for the Propagation of the Gospel, Elias Neau, remarked, "I have been told that the Negroes bear on their foreheads the marks of the reprobation and that their color and their condition [enslavement] confirms that opinion."[15] In fact, much of the antislavery literature as well as the literature of those wishing to "Christianize" the enslaved Africans had to include "apologies and extenuations" of the enslaved's color in an effort to counter arguments that the dark color was a sign of inhumanity.

If a studied and conscious ideology of Black inferiority began in the United States as a rationale for slavery, it would later become the justification for postemancipation practices of White supremacy in general. George Fredrickson explains:

> The attitudes that underlay the belief that the Negro was doomed by nature itself to perpetual slavishness and subordination to the whites were not new, nor was the doctrine itself if considered as a popular belief that lacked intellectual respectability; but when asserted dogmatically and with an aura of philosophical authority, ...it became, for the first time, the basis of a world view, an explicit ideology around which the beneficiaries of white supremacy could organize themselves and their thoughts.[16]

Essentially, whiteness — whether determined by ethnicity or biology — emerged in America, even as it had in Europe, as a mark of human superiority. It was viewed as the normative and certainly most valued human characteristic. As such, it was a central factor for holding together a once motley throng of European people, even as it became a measure for denigrating other human beings. This contemptuous White group identity in America was the harbinger of White culture.

The Efficacy of White Culture

White culture is not marked by its uniquely creative and enriching social contributions. Rather, it is distinguished by its ability to promote the sanctity of whiteness by devaluing that which is non-White. This culture asserts the supremacy of whiteness and is accompanied by social, political, and economic systems that also privilege whiteness. Whiteness has become, therefore, the ticket to social, political, and economic status, if not power, in American society. White culture with its secretion of White supremacist values and ideology serves as a safeguard for a White, racist, patriarchal hegemony in America.

It should be noted that some White people, though recognizing White hegemony, refute the existence of White culture. White Americans sometimes disavow it in an effort to escape responsibility for its vile nature. They denounce its existence, yet they continue to benefit from the varied privileges of being "White." Others deny the existence of White culture for more judicious reasons. One such person is political theorist Manning Marable.

Reflecting the Marxist philosophy that influences his thought, a philosophy that typically minimizes the value of culture in favor of class/economic categories, Marable argues:

> To be white in the United States says nothing directly about an individual culture, ethnic heritage, or biological background. A society created to preserve "white culture" either would be very confused or tremendously disappointed. White culture does not exist. White power, privileges, and prerogatives within capitalist society do exist.[17]

Although he does not admit a White culture, Marable does acknowledge whiteness as a "racial" identity. Race, he says, is an "artificial social construction" deliberately imposed upon people in order to secure exploitation. Race, according to Marable, indicates "an unequal relationship between social aggregates." In this regard, whiteness as a racial identity is a mark of privilege. Marable elaborates:

> Whiteness is fundamentally a statement of the continued pattern of exploitation of subordinated racial groups which create economic surpluses for privileged groups. To be white means that one's "life chances"... improve dramatically.... Whiteness was fundamentally a measure of personal privilege and power, not a cultural statement.[18]

Marable is correct in establishing whiteness as a "measure" of privilege and power, while also emphasizing that White Americans represent various cultural backgrounds. Yet to deny the existence of a White culture is to ignore the various marks of culture that usher forth from whiteness. If culture is "the totality of any given society's way of life" and "comprises a people's total social heritage, including language, ideas, habits, beliefs, customs, social organization and traditions, arts and symbolism, crafts and artifacts,"[19] then a White culture is certainly operative in the United States. It has become virtually synonymous with American culture, as it negatively juxtaposes White/American culture with that which is non-White. For instance, "classical" American music, literature, and art typically reflect European roots or White American preferences, suggesting an inferior status to non-Euro/non-White art forms. The symbols of beauty in White/American culture also bespeak whiteness. Standard language reflects White cultural values. For instance, words associated with blackness customarily signify evil and badness. Words associated with whiteness are commonly an indicator of purity and goodness. Given the preponderance of cultural markers, it would seem precipitous to deny the existence of a White culture.

Though it may be considered degenerate, destructive, oppositional, or indistinct, White culture is real. It permeates American society. To disavow it precludes a thorough analysis of White racism. White culture is the very culture that harbors and nurtures White racism. Built on a false premise of superiority, if not a specious foundation of national identity, White culture functions to secure White supremacy. It sustains White power.

Recognizing the validity of Marable's observation concerning the diversity of cultures that comprise White America, it is important, however, to clarify that not everything issuing from White America (such as research, literature, music, visual arts, and so on) is necessarily a reflection of White culture. White Americans can choose not to affirm and not to perpetuate White culture. They can renounce the unmerited social, political, and economic privileges of whiteness as well as acknowledge the inhumane nature of White culture. More especially, White Americans can renounce if not diminish the power of White culture by doing at least three things: (1) self-critically reclaim their cultural heritage and historical struggles that occurred prior to their becoming White in America; (2) take responsibility for the "price" of shameless privilege and arrogant elitism they have paid to be White in America; and (3) accept culpability for the inexorable "price" non-Whites have been forced to pay to ensure the primacy of whiteness in America. Realizing that White culture has "choked many a human being to death," James Baldwin offers this redemptive possibility for White Americans: "Go back to where you started, or as far as you can, examine all of it, travel your road again and tell the truth about it. Sing or shout or testify or keep it to yourself: but *know when you came.*"[20]

Notwithstanding the fact that White culture is not necessarily synonymous with White America, the vibrant reality of this nefarious culture simply cannot be denied. This is a culture that continues to be sustained by its uncanny ability to dehumanize and denigrate non-White peoples. It is a destructive force in people's lives, especially the lives of Black people. It is, in fact, White culture's disparaging nature that demands the virulent exploitation of Black sexuality. Let us now then turn to the role of sexuality in White culture.

SEXUALITY IN CULTURE

While "the master's tools will never dismantle the master's house," as Audre Lorde rightly points out,[21] prudent use of the master's tools may certainly help one to understand the subtleties of the master's house. It is for this reason that Michel Foucault's analysis of sexuality and power is valuable to my project. Though Foucault's analyses sometimes reflect a self-serving androcentric perspective (as many feminist scholars have noted), they provide an "insider's" view of White patriarchal culture. From the vantage point of those who are most often dominant in society, Foucault provides a meticulous analysis of social power. His analysis clarifies the role of sexuality in society and culture and, in so doing, indicates why the violation of Black sexuality is basic to White culture. We will now examine Foucault's analysis in some detail so to comprehend fully the intricate connections between White power and Black sexuality.

Foucault on Power

Power, Foucault argues, is not a unitary, centralized force. It is not concentrated in the state or any single institution. Rather, power is exercised on all levels of society where people relate with each other. Power is always relational: "It is created in the relationships which sustain it."[22] Foucault thus speaks of "power relations."

Power relations are not imposed upon people from above. They emerge from below. They are part of a mosaic of the way people interact with one another as families, lovers, workers, and so on. The types of relationships individuals form in their complex web of interactions with others shape the types of institutions and structures that emerge in society. For instance, unequal relationships lead to structures of domination. Feminist theorist Jana Sawicki explains that "Foucault's 'bottom-up' analysis of power is an attempt to show how power relations at the microlevel of society make possible certain global effects of domination, such as class power and patriarchy."[23]

Essentially, Foucault places the origins of power relations in the hands of "the people." Though he recognizes that there are dominating agents of power, he does not consign power to any one agent. He perceives power as being everywhere but always ascending from the bottom. This conception of power suggests two means for eliminating structures of domination. The first is to change the web of interpersonal interactions, beginning at the bottom. If the way persons relate to one another on the microlevels of society is altered, then the way power is institutionalized will also be changed.

A second mechanism for change is intrinsic to power itself. Foucault argues that power includes its own resistance. Wherever power is exercised, there is an attempt to be freed from that power, whether it is the child in relation to the parent, the student to the teacher, or the worker to the employer. In relations of power, resistance is inevitable. In terms of societal change, this suggests that if those engaged in resistance on their various fronts coalesced their resistance activities, then they could possibly change the web of relationships that leads to dominating and oppressive structures. Foucault says:

> Where there is power, there is resistance.... [A relationship of power] depends on a multiplicity of points of resistance: these play the role of adversary, target, support, or handle in power relations. These points of resistance are present everywhere in the power network. Hence there is no single locus of great Refusal, no soul of revolt, source of all rebellions, or pure law of the revolutionary. Instead there is a plurality of resistances.... And it is doubtless the strategic codification of these points of resistance that makes a revolution possible, somewhat similar to the way in which the state relies on the institutional integration of power relationships.[24]

Contrary to what some feminists and others suggest, it seems that Foucault has not mystified but demystified the idea of power and domination. He has done this by placing the origins of power in the hands of people and by suggesting that change begins with altering patterns of interpersonal relationships. Sawicki notes, "The practical implication of [Foucault's] model is that resistance must be carried out in local struggles against the many forms of power exercised at the everyday level of social relations."[25]

While there is no doubt a danger of overemphasizing the microlevels of power to the point of ignoring the very real structures of domination that shape people's lives, Foucault has judiciously placed the responsibility for the kind of society in which we live *back* in the hands of those who have shaped and formed that society. He has held *people* — not impersonal or sometimes elusive structures of domination — accountable for the sexism, racism, classism, and heterosexism that terrorize much of our world.

Foucault's "bottom-up" approach to understanding power and its resistance should be especially noted because it will become particularly germane to the latter part of this study when we explore a womanist response to the difficulties surrounding Black people's sexuality. But for now, as we seek to understand the significance of Black sexuality for White culture, let us further examine what Foucault says about the exercise of power.

Foucault stresses that power is neither coercive nor repressive. It is disciplinary and productive. Power's disciplinary character is that which exercises constraints over the body and conscience of individuals. It compels people to behave in certain ways. It obliges them to adhere to certain societal and personal standards, that is, norms, rules, regulations, values, and mores. This kind of power rewards those who do adhere to these standards by integrating them into the mainstream of society. It grants them at least the opportunity to secure all the rights and privileges of the "bourgeois." Those who are judged as nonconforming do not merit inclusion into society's mainstream. Instead, they are ostracized, alienated, marginalized, and even punished through legal and extralegal methods. According to Foucault, it is this disciplinary power that causes persons to be labeled as criminal, insane, immoral, perverts, deviants, and so on. Penal and mental health institutions are an outgrowth of exercising disciplinary power.

In order for disciplinary power to be realized, however, people must be made aware of the "rules and regulations" of society. They must feel constrained to behave in a certain manner privately as well as publicly. Power's realization is its productive character.

Power is realized through the production of certain forms of knowledge — a process Foucault calls the "will to knowledge" — and the careful deployment of this knowledge through public discourse. Discursive power is crucial to Foucault's analysis. What is considered proper or improper conduct, licit or illicit behavior, is communicated through discourse. Such social discourse is transmitted through educational, family, religious, and other social institutions. Discourse has two interrelated tasks. It not only establishes proper conduct, but in so doing implies that those who fall outside of acceptable behavioral standards are at best pariahs, at worst inferior beings. Foucault puts it simply, "Discourse transmits and produces power; it reinforces it."[26] This brings us to the role of sexuality in the exercise of power.

Sexual Discourse

"How is it that in a society like ours," Foucault asks, "sexuality is not simply a means of reproducing the species, the family, and the individual? Not simply a means to obtain pleasure and enjoyment? How has sexuality come to be considered the privileged place where our deepest 'truth' is read and expressed?"[27] Foucault discerned that this is so because sexuality is integral to power. It is the axis where the human body and reproduction come together. Power can be exerted over a people through careful regulation of their bodies, their perceptions of their bodies, and their reproductive capacities. Such regulation and hence exercise of power can be achieved through the conscientious deployment of sexuality, manipulating how persons view their sexuality, primarily through discourse. Foucault makes clear that sexual discourse is one of the most effective mediums through which power is exercised.

Foucault further notes the importance of sexuality to the maintenance of power. He points out that sexuality is a mechanism by which distinctions can be made between classes and groups of people. To question or impugn the sexuality of another bolsters one's own claims to superiority as it suggests another group's inferiority. Again, if one can establish that a people's sexual behavior is improper, then one can also suggest that that people is inferior.

Proficient management of sexual discourse can easily foster this type of domination and demonization. Foucault clarifies the role of sexuality and sexual discourse in the exercise of power when he explains, "The deployment of sexuality has its reason for being, not in reproducing itself, but in proliferating, innovating, annexing, creating, and penetrating bodies in an increasingly detailed way, in controlling populations in an increasingly comprehensive way."[28] An attack upon a people's sexuality becomes important, then, because sexuality implies one's very humanity. It involves a person's self-image, specifically the way an individual defines her or his femininity or masculinity and the way a person regards her or his physiognomy. Sexuality also involves one's reproductive capacity. Therefore, to malign a people's sexuality is to call in question their very humanity. And to control a people's reproductive capacity — which can be done by direct assaults upon their sexual activity or by indirect assaults through manipulating their self-concept — is of course to control their population. When one understands the role of sexuality in White people's maintenance of power, then one can understand the significance of Black sexuality to White culture.

Black Sexuality in White Culture

It is necessary for White society to control Black people's sexuality, meaning their bodies and reproductive capacities, so as to control them as a people. It is also necessary to impugn Black sexuality in order to suggest that Black people are inferior beings. As argued earlier in this chapter, White culture exists primarily as it is contrasted with that which is non-White. It is a culture maintained by an ideology of White supremacy while at the same time it secretes this ideology. If this ideological foundation were to be "authoritatively" refuted, then the foundation of White culture would be deeply shaken. With the fall of White culture would come the collapse of White patriarchal hegemony in America. The omnipotence of White culture is crucial to the continuance of American society as we know it. Likewise critical to White culture's existence is its ability to avow White superiority by asserting — seemingly "by any means necessary" — the inferiority of non-White peoples. And, as Foucault firmly argues, there is no better way to impugn the character and humanity of a people than by maligning their sexuality.

If the exploitation of non-White sexuality in general is important to White culture, then the abuse of Black sexuality in particular is absolutely critical. Black sexuality has been the primary target of White culture for at least two reasons. First, Black people have been absolutely critical to White economic power, initially as free labor and later as cheap labor. The ability to freely exploit Black bodies with relative impunity has been critical to the labor market. To that end, White culture has attacked Black sexuality as a means of dehumanizing Black men and women. Such dehumanization has made it easier to enslave Black people and to treat them merely as property and labor commodities rather than as human beings.

The second reason for White culture's inordinate attention to Black sexuality has to do with Black people's very color and physiognomy. As suggested earlier, nothing opposes whiteness more radically than blackness. Even Black people's physical features, such as hair texture, facial features, and body type, seem to radically counter those of White people. In addition, African cultures and ways of living are very differ-ent from European cultures and ways of life. These grave differences have inevitably bred White people's fascination with and fear of Black people. Such fascination and fear have seemed to only heighten the sense that Black people have to be controlled. Any persons who stirred such intense emotion in White people were certainly dangerous to White people's sense of superiority and indeed to the preservation of White culture and White hegemony. Again, the best way to gain control of non-White people while protecting White hegemonic val-ues has been to attack their sexuality. Cornel West puts the matter plainly, "White supremacist ideology is based first and foremost on the degradation of black bodies in order to control them."[29]

But Patricia Hill Collins perhaps explains it best when she says:

> Privileged groups define their alleged sexual practices as the myth-ical norm and label sexual practices and groups who diverge from this norm as deviant and threatening. Maintaining the norm of the financially independent, white middle-class family organized around a monogamous heterosexual couple requires stigmatizing African-American families as being deviant, and a primary source of this assumed deviancy stems from allegations about Black sexuality.... Differences in sexuality thus take on more mean-ing than just benign sexual variation. Each individual becomes a powerful conduit for social relations of domination whereby indi-vidual anxieties, fears and doubts about sexuality can be annexed by larger systems of oppression.[30]

Essentially, when looked at from the perspective of White people's ability to exercise power over non-White peoples, Black sexuality be-comes a fundamental mark of White culture. The sexual politics of White culture reflects the nature of the culture itself. It is a politic that systematically devalues the sexuality of non-White people, espe-cially Black people, for the sheer purpose of controlling them and hence promoting White supremacy. Historiographers John D'Emilio and Estelle Freedman affirm this very fact as they note that by the seventeenth century, sexuality had taken shape "as a powerful means by which white Americans maintained dominance over people of other races."[31] So why, then, borrowing from Foucault's query, has Black sexuality become an obsession of White culture and society, rather than simply a means of production and source of pleasure for Black people? Because it is a linchpin in the sustenance of White power in America.

Sexuality and the Christian Tradition

As significant as it is to understand the relation of sexuality to power, it is also crucial to understand Christianity's role in giving sexuality such authoritative prominence in the denigration of particular human beings. Western Christianity's dominant approach to sexuality has contributed to White culture's ability to challenge Black people's humanity by impugning their sexuality. This approach is grounded in a dubious separation made between the body and the spirit.

Pre-Christian Hebrew life showed little tendency toward seeing the body as an impediment to spirituality. Sexuality apparently was appreciated as a gift from God, as evidenced by the Hebrew scriptural references to persons as flesh rather than spirit or by the celebration of sensuality in the Song of Solomon. Yet Christianity gradually became influenced by those aspects of Greek thought that denigrated the body and fostered a profound split between the body and the spirit. This "spiritualistic dualism" was primarily crafted by Platonic and neo-Platonic thought.

According to Platonism the real world of value and beauty was that which could be perceived only by the soul. This world was conceived as timeless, changeless, and immaterial. The body and its senses could not grasp such a world. To appreciate this world, therefore, one had to essentially deny bodily pleasures and activities, including sexual activity, and strive for a more contemplative, ascetic life.

Also greatly influencing early Christian thought was the Stoic philosophy of Rome, articulated most prominently by Seneca, a contemporary of Jesus. The fundamental axiom of Stoic philosophy was to "live according to nature." Nature was identified with divine order, which was, in turn, identified with reason. This was in keeping with the Stoic idea of God as *logos*, or reason. To live according to nature (meaning, reason) was to achieve union with God.

With reason identified with nature, the adversary in Stoic philosophy was that which was most opposed to reason/nature: emotion and passion. So a depreciation of the body, the home of the irrational passions of "man," was called for, along with the emphasis on reason and the mind. The lack of appreciation for human passion had strong implications for sexuality. Sexual activity in and of itself was not bad, but passion was viewed as very dubious. Sex was viewed as corrupt when it emerged from passion. This meant that the only rational use for sexual activity was procreation.

It was into this Greco-Roman world of dualistic philosophy that Christianity entered. There is perhaps no Christian thinker more significantly influenced by the dualistic thinking of Platonism, neo-Platonism, and Stoicism than Augustine of Hippo, who subsequently had a tremendous impact on Christian thought. Neo-Platonism offered Augustine "a vision of eternal truth and a call to turn away from sensual pleasures and purify his soul."[32]

As reflected by his own personal struggles, Augustine was disturbed by the problem of sexual lust and passion and was most concerned about the "genital aspects" of human sexuality. For him, human sexuality had been contaminated by lust with the fall of Adam. Prior to the fall, Augustine argued, every part of Adam's body was perfectly obedient to God's will. Pre-fall sexual relations were not seen as sinful because they were a controlled act performed by humans to procreate. But after the fall, Adam lost control of his will. A sign of this was his loss of control over his body and body parts, specifically his genitalia. The involuntary movements of sexual organs (such as male erections) were the first sign of this loss of control and, hence, disobedience to God. Thereafter, sexual activity was no longer a controlled act for procreation, but, instead, became a "kind of spasm" in which reason is completely overtaken by passion. Augustine describes sexual activity motivated by passion as an act where "at the crisis of excitement it practically paralyzes all power of deliberate thought."[33]

Augustine's views on sexuality are generally characteristic of early Christian attitudes. St. Thomas Aquinas, for instance, proposed during the late Middle Ages a "threefold standard" for sexual acts: they must be done for the right purpose (procreation), with the right person (one's spouse), and in the right way (heterosexual genital intercourse). Even during the sixteenth century the Protestant Reformation did not redeem sexuality as it remained singularly identified with the lustful urges of the body. Martin Luther, for instance, believed that sexual activity was a strong, lustful human urge. Marriage for him was a necessity so as to allow for some controlled response to this libidinal urge. John

Calvin was less cynical about sex because he did believe that it had some constructive effects. Nevertheless, he thought that even within marriage it needed to be constrained by the rigid bounds of "delicacy and propriety."

Given the churches' historical attitudes on sexuality issues, Carter Heyward aptly observes that "the christian church has been the chief architect of an attitude toward sexuality during the last seventeen-hundred years of European and Euroamerican history — an obsessive, proscriptive attitude."[34]

While Foucault would not necessarily disagree with Heyward's observations concerning the church and sexuality, he does go to great lengths to point out that this is an inherited attitude. Foucault accurately notes, "We must concede that Christianity did not invent this code of sexual behavior. Christianity accepted it, reinforced it, and gave it a much larger and more widespread strength than it had before. But the so-called Christian morality is nothing more than a piece of pagan ethics inserted into Christianity."[35] Foucault, however, does give Christianity credit for innovating a profound way in which persons view sexual activity. Sexuality became for Christianity one means for exploring the truth of one's self. "Christianity," explains Foucault, "proposed a new type of experience of oneself as a sexual being."[36] Yet while Christianity may have made people aware of who they were as sexual beings, it did so in a negative way. The dominant Christian thought regarding human sexuality emphasized it as something that Christian women and men should strive to overcome so that they could live a life more pleasing to God.

It should also be noted that the dualistic philosophies that governed the church's tradition in terms of sexuality were also intrinsically misogynistic and have reflected a "patriarchal dualism."[37] In other words "spiritualistic dualism" is inherently sexist. Women have been consistently associated with the body, passion, and the irrational, while men have been associated with the soul, reason, and rationality. While pre-Christian Hebrew thought may not have contributed to the denigration of human flesh, it certainly laid the foundation for the demonizing of women's sexuality. As biblical scholar Renita Weems notes, the prophets in particular contributed in large measure to the notion that "women's sexuality is deviant, evil, and dangerous."[38] Following in this line of thought, one of the early church fathers, Tertullian, went as far as to suggest that women were "the devil's gateway." Pettus Damiani, an eleventh-century monk, described women as "bait of Satan, by-product of paradise, poison in our food, source of sin, temptresses, whores of lust, sirens, and chief witches."[39] John McNeil sums up the misogynistic character of the early church writings:

> The Fathers frequently repeat Aristotle's dictum that "the woman is a mutilated male" and agree with his position that the male is by nature superior and the female inferior; the one rules and the other is ruled. There is a tendency to identify the male principle with the soul and the female principle with the body. Woman is naturally subject to man because in man the direction of reason is greater. This went hand in hand with a sexual interpretation of original sin, with Eve symbolizing all women as the evil protagonist.[40]

Ethicist James Nelson also explains:

> The alienation of spirit from body, of reason from emotions, of "higher life" from "fleshly life" found both impetus and expression in the subordination of women. Men assumed to themselves superiority in reason and spirit and thus believed themselves destined to lead both civil and religious communities. Contrarily, women were identified with the traits of emotion, body, and sensuality. Their monthly "pollutions" were taken as a sign of religious uncleanness and emotional instability.[41]

Yet the portrait of women in spiritualistic dualism is not strictly one-dimensional. Women have also been cast as chaste virgins. Given women's role as mothers and wives, it would not do to cast women as irrevocably evil. Such an evil being would have a corrupting influence over children and a certain seductive power over men, as Eve was thought to have over Adam. Therefore, women were further caricatured by a denial of their sexuality. The "perfect" woman was cast as a combination of Mary — virginal, pure, and submissive — and one willing to produce children for her man. Rosemary Ruether sums up the Christian legacy of "patriarchal dualism":

> The male ideology of the "feminine" that we have inherited in the West seems to be rooted in a self-alienated experience of the body and the world, project[ed] upon the lower half of these dualisms.... It is always woman who is the "other," the antithesis over against which one defines "authentic" (male) selfhood.[42]

As we will see in more detail later, while the woman may "always" have been relegated to the "lower half" of the dualisms, it is certainly not *only* she. This Western Christian tradition has also influenced White cultural dispositions toward Black people. They too would be viewed as the antithesis of "authentic selfhood" (meaning whiteness). They too would be relegated to the lower half of the dualisms, so that "spiritualistic dualism" would provide a sacred canopy not only for sexism but also for racism. This means that Black women would become at least doubly victimized, thoroughly entrapped by a sexist and racist sacred dualistic ideology that implied their inhumanity.

Essentially, the Western Christian tradition opened wide the door for the possibility of utilizing sexual practices, or alleged sexual practices, as a means for devaluing and demonizing human beings. It did this in several ways. First, it tended to make genital sexual activity the defining feature of sexuality. Therefore, maligning the sexual ethics of a particular people became sufficient in a Christian society for challenging their entire personhood. Second, by associating sexual activity with passionate, irrational, and even satanic behavior, the Christian tradition provided persons with a means for placing a sacred canopy over their acts of domination and oppression. For if one can show that a people was by nature libidinous, then it was not difficult to suggest that such a people was by nature an affront to God. Finally, the Christian tradition's "spiritualistic dualism" alienated persons from their sexuality as it demanded the denial of their body-selves. Such alienation from an essential part of one's being often compels one to project onto others what one finds undesirable, but unavoidable, about oneself. In this regard, those who view themselves as superior in society (with White men generally at the apex) are compelled to deny their "vile" sexuality and project their own very real sexual desires on others, thus labeling those others as hypersexual. In short, the historically dominant Christian attitude toward sexuality provided the ruling class with an effective tool for justifying its domination over others.

CONCLUSIONS

This chapter has attempted to show that White society's preoccupation with Black women's and men's sexuality *is* about more than fascination and fear. It has to do with maintaining the status quo of White power in American society. Foucault's analysis of sexual politics and an appreciation for Christianity's stance in regard to sexuality clarify why vilification of Black sexuality has enabled White people to maintain control over Black bodies as well as to uphold false notions of White supremacy. The next chapter explores in some detail the particular assaults on Black sexuality that have been germane to the existence of White hegemony and have impacted Black people's attitudes toward sexually related concerns.

CHAPTER 2

Stereotypes, False Images, Terrorism
The White Assault upon Black Sexuality

Carnal, passionate, lustful, lewd, rapacious, bestial, sensual — these are just some of the many terms that come to mind when thinking of the ways in which White culture has depicted Black people's sexuality. This practice of dehumanizing Black people by maligning their sexuality has been a decisive factor in the exercise of White power in America. So crucial is the exploitation of Black sexuality to White dominance that White culture has left almost no stone unturned in its violation of Black bodies and intimacy. This violation has been grounded in numerous sexually charged stereotypes. These stereotypes have been critical to the achievement of unprincipled racist power. By disguising and mystifying objective reality, they have been indispensable to the maintenance of the social, political, and economic status quo in America. They have functioned to make White supremacy appear not only necessary but also "natural, normal and an inevitable part of everyday life."[1] At the same time, these sexual stereotypes have impacted Black lives in such a way as to render sexuality a virtually taboo topic for the Black church and community.

But how, precisely, has this been accomplished? What has been the nature of the stereotypes? What type of assault has it been, that Black people still suffer from its blows?

This chapter will attempt to answer these questions by looking at selected stereotypes and the concomitant racist images that surround Black people's sexuality. It will also highlight the inevitable consequences of these stereotypes: vicious attacks upon Black bodies. Since most of these racist caricatures were developed in order to justify the institution of slavery, this chapter will focus on the emergence and efficacy of these stereotypes during the slavery era.

31

It should be noted, however, that not all of the many stereotypes concerning Black sexuality are explored. This chapter examines only those that have been particularly germane to White hegemony in American society. The crucial role that the degradation of Black sexuality plays in White culture is consistently stressed because it accounts, in part, for the centrality that Black sexual stereotypes have in White culture, as well as for the perseverance of these stereotypes. By penetrating the conundrum of sexual images that White racism has foisted upon Black people, we should be even closer to appreciating Black people's complex reactions to sexual issues.

THE ROOTS OF THE ATTACK

While slavery is certainly the cauldron out of which demeaning attacks on Black sexuality were formed, these attacks were grounded in ideologies and attitudes that preceded the slavery era. They were rooted in Europeans' first encounters with Africans. During these encounters (as mentioned in the previous chapter), Europeans were often struck by the stark differences in appearance between themselves and Africans. They were also impressed by the differences in customs, rituals, religion, and basic way of life. Winthrop Jordan notes that early travelers to Africa "rarely failed to comment upon [skin complexion] and then moved on to dress (or rather lack of it) and manners."[2] One sixteenth-century traveler wrote: "These people are all blacke, and are called Negros, without apparell, saving before their privities."[3]

Unfortunately, these first impressions did not excite an appreciation for human diversity. Instead, they nourished a disgust with, if not fear of, difference. This aversion for Africans gave way to various perverted myths. The differences in appearance, dress, religion, and manner of living converged to give rise to new notions — as well as no doubt to support already existing notions — that Africans were an extremely libidinous people. An Englishman wrote in his journal of travels to Africa:

> They have no knowledge of God; those that traffique and are conversant among strange Countrey people are civiller than the common sort of people, they are very greedie eaters, and no lesse drinkers, and very lecherous, and theevish, and much addicted to uncleanenesse: one man hath as many wives as hee is able to keepe and maintaine.[4]

One especially despicable myth fabricated by European travelers to Africa involved apes. Englishmen easily drew comparisons between the sexual habits of these animals and those of Africans. One sixteenth-century writer on the subject advanced that "Men that have low and flat nostrils [that is, the Africans] are Libidinous as Apes that attempt women."[5] Even more perverse stories developed as European intruders into Africa alleged actual sexual contact between apes and African women. One John Atkins wrote:

> At some Places the *Negroes* have been suspected of Bestiality with them [apes and monkeys], and by the Boldness and Affection they are known under some Circumstances to express to our Females; the Ignorance and Stupidity on the other side, to guide or control Lust; but more from the near resemblances are sometimes met to the Human Species would tempt one to suspect the Fact.[6]

Jordan explains the reason for such obscene mythology: "By forging a sexual link between Negroes and apes . . . , Englishmen were able to give vent to their feelings that Negroes were lewd, lascivious and wanton people."[7]

Myths such as those just noted concerning Africans' sexual deviance were well established in European culture by the time the Europeans invaded America. But again, it would be during the slavery era that these myths would take on the peculiarities of White culture and that specific White cultural stereotypes concerning Black men and women would form. The success of the institution of slavery demanded dehumanizing stereotypes of the enslaved human beings. With an urgent need to disengage the "Negro" from his or her humanity, White culture mounted a vigorous attack upon Black sexuality.

SLAVERY AND BLACK SEXUALITY

The stereotypes and images of slavery regarding Black sexuality have been tenacious. They reflect the core of the White cultural assault upon Black bodies and intimacy even as they continue to impact Black lives. There is no better story by which to begin our exploration of these particular stereotypes and images than that of Sarah Bartmann. Though Sarah Bartmann's story occurred outside the actual parameters of American slavery, it epitomizes the nature and complexity of the White cultural attack upon Black women and men.

•

In 1810 one Sarah Bartmann, a Black South African woman, also known as the "Hottentot Venus," caused a "scandal" in London when she was exhibited "to the public in a manner offensive to decency."[8] In the early nineteenth century, Sarah Bartmann was a circuslike attraction across Europe. Her naked body was displayed so that Europeans could gaze upon one particular aspect of her physiognomy, her protruding buttocks. After five years of this dehumanizing exhibition, Sarah Bartmann died in Paris at the age of twenty-five. Her degradation, however, continued long after her death. An autopsy was performed on her, with particular attention being paid to her genitalia. The autopsy was prepared "in a way so as to allow one to see the nature of the labia."[9] As in life, also in death, Ms. Bartmann went on display. Her genitalia became the topic of many a medical article. In 1817, Dr. George Cuvier drew meticulous comparisons between Ms. Bartmann's genitalia and that of an orangutan. "Sarah Bartmann's sexual parts, her genitalia and her buttocks [would] serve as the central image for the black female throughout the nineteenth century."[10] They would also come to an undignified rest in the Musée de l'Homme in Paris, where they remained on display far after the nineteenth century.[11]

The treatment of Sarah Bartmann points to the manner in which White culture studiously demeaned Black sexuality in its efforts to dehumanize Black men and women. First of all, it reveals how this culture relied on the "authority of science" to support its stereotypes by providing "evidence" that Black people were biologically predisposed to being lascivious and sexually perverse. As in the case of Sarah Bartmann, studies were conducted upon the genitalia of Black people, especially Black women. Reminiscent of the early European assumptions, these studies generally concluded that Black men and women had more in common physically and biologically with apes than with other human beings. Such findings continued to call into question Black people's ability to be anything but wanton creatures.

As suggested by Foucault's analysis of sexual politics, the gathering of dubious scientific data is essential if not inevitable in the exercise of power. Such "will to knowledge" provides the necessary "power knowledge" to justify the inequitable exercise of power over other human beings. In this instance, the "power knowledge" of White culture provided the "scientific evidence" necessary to depict Black people as sexual deviants and anomalies, and thus as inferior beings.

The treatment of Sarah Bartmann further suggests the perhaps subtle role of the Christian tradition in the attack upon Black sexuality. The depiction of Sarah Bartmann is representative of the manner in which Black men and women were to be depicted by White culture. They were portrayed as lustful and passionate beings. That such a nature served as sufficient proof of Black people's inferiority, and thus their need to be dominated by White people, no doubt reflects the influence of the Western Christian tradition, which condemned human sexuality as evil. To be sure, this tradition would influence White cultural disposition toward Black people. To suggest that Black people were oversexualized meant that they were governed by matters of the flesh. This alone, according to the dominant early Christian tradition, was enough to signal their inferiority and need to be dominated by those governed by reason, namely, White men.

As suggested earlier, this portended double trouble for Black females. If women and Blacks were considered overly sensual people, then Black women did not stand a chance of being treated with dignity or respect. They were embodiments of both a condemned gender and a condemned race. It is then no wonder that Sarah Bartmann could be displayed throughout Europe with no serious opposition coming forth to stop her abuse. This leads us to the final and perhaps most significant aspect of the White cultural attack upon Black sexuality suggested by the Sarah Bartmann story.

BLACK WOMEN: A GATEWAY TO DEPRAVITY

The prominence of Sarah Bartmann suggests the centrality of Black women to the success of White culture. Since women in general are held in such low regard by White patriarchal society, it is a logical conclusion for this culture to blame Black women for Black depravity. To reiterate, White culture serves to protect a White *patriarchal* hegemony. It is as sexist as it is racist. Black women are victimized by both of these cultural dispositions. They personify the intersection of race and gender interests. Deborah Gray White explains:

> The uniqueness of the African-American female's situation is that she stands at the crossroads of two of the most well-developed ideologies in America, that regarding women and that regarding the Negro....
>
> The black woman's position at the nexus of America's sex and race mythology has made it most difficult for her to escape the mythology.[12]

Vulnerable to both the racist and sexist ideologies of White culture, Black women provide the gateway for the White cultural assault upon Black sexuality. Recognizing this, Patricia Hill Collins says, "Examining the links between sexuality and power in a system of interlocking race, gender, and class oppression should reveal how important controlling Black women's sexuality has been to the effective operation of domination overall."[13] Essentially, the treatment of Black women has become the basis for the exercise of White power over Black bodies. As Robert Staples points out, "in no other area [are] there . . . so many stereotypes and myths [as in] that of Black female sexuality."[14]

Stereotypes and false images surrounding Black female sexuality provide the foundation for sexual exploitation and humiliation of Black men, as well as for fostering notions of White male and female superiority. Some of these stereotypes and images have been so insidious that they continue to influence Black people's responses to sexual issues. Let us now look more closely at the particular White cultural stereotypes and adjoining images that have had a predominant impact upon Black people, appropriately beginning with those concerning Black women.

The Jezebel

One of the most prominent stereotypes has characterized the Black female as "a person governed almost entirely by her libido." She has been described as having an insatiable sexual appetite, being extraordinarily passionate, and being sexually aggressive and cunning. Such stereotyping has produced the paramount image for Black womanhood in White culture — the Jezebel image. "Jezebel" has come to symbolize an evil, scheming, and seductive woman. This symbol no doubt owes its meaning to the ninth-century Phoenician princess and wife of the Israelite king Ahab, who was accused of destroying the kingdom with her idolatrous practices and otherwise diabolical ways (1 Kings 16:29–22:53).

Though the Jezebel image in relation to Black women would come to fruition during slavery, like White cultural stereotypes and images of Black people in general, it is rooted in European travels to Africa. Travelers often interpreted African women's sparse dress — dress appropriate to the climate of Africa — as a sign of their lewdness and lack of chastity. White explains: "The idea that black women were exceptionally sensual first gained credence when Englishmen went to Africa to buy slaves. Unaccustomed to the requirements of tropical climate,

Europeans mistook seminudity for lewdness."[15] Indeed, the warm climate came to be associated with "hot constition'd Ladies" possessed of a temper "hot and lascivious."[16]

If the habits, way of life, and living conditions of the African woman gave birth to the notion that Black women were Jezebels, then the conditions and exigencies of slavery brought it to maturity. The life situation of the enslaved woman encouraged the idea that she was a Jezebel, even as the Jezebel image served to justify the life situation she was forced to endure. Essentially, the very institution that the Jezebel image served to guard gave credence to the idea that Black women were in fact Jezebels.

For instance, the institution of slavery forced Black women to display their bodies in a manner that was considered contrary to antebellum notions of moral, chaste, and decent women. This was an era when a "proper" lady was marked not only by her innocence, her attention to her home, and the moral upbringing of her children, but also by her manner of dress. Clothing signified one's moral status as well as class. A "respectable" White woman was thus "adorned" in layers of clothing. By contrast, the enslaved female was often given barely enough clothing to cover her body. In addition, the enslaved woman's work in the fields often required her to raise her dress above her knees. Even house servants often had to pull their skirts up to polish and wash floors. Their sparse covering coupled with working in a manner that required that they were even more exposed all fed the sentiment that the Black female was a wanton, loose creature.

Further supporting the Jezebel image was the public display of nudity that slavery often required. Like Sarah Bartmann, enslaved females' bodies were often stripped bare as they were closely examined, poked, and prodded during slave auctions and sales. Numerous slave testimonies witness to this fact. One enslaved person recalled in an interview:

> Each slave, whether female or male, is brought up to the block, and sometimes stripped entirely of all clothing, that the buyer may examine as to any bodily defect, and their persons are handled like oxen or horses, and each is sold separately to the highest bidder.[17]

A person enslaved in Missouri remembered, "Right here in St. Louis men and women have been stripped stark naked and examined by the critical eyes of prospective purchasers as though they were dumb driven cattle."[18] Lu Perkins said, "I'members when they put me on the auction block. They pulled my dress down over my back to my waist, to show I ain't gashed and slashed up."[19]

Adding to the degradation of public nudity, Black females were sometimes taken to a space where their sexual organs could be closely examined by their prospective buyer so that he (sometimes she) could determine her suitability for breeding. Again, such exigencies of slavery only catered to the notion that Black women were Jezebels. Certainly, in the irrational logic of White culture, no self-respecting woman would allow herself to be put on display in such a manner.

In addition to the conditions of dress and bodily display, the Jezebel image was also reinforced because the reproductive capacity of enslaved women was often a topic of public conversation. With the disruption of the slave trade, the growth of the enslaved population was dependent upon the fertility of the already enslaved. This meant that some masters "encouraged" — by a variety of despicable means — frequent pregnancies of the enslaved women. Hillardy Yellerday recalls from her days of enslavement:

> When a girl became a woman, she was required to go to a man and become a mother.... Master would sometimes go and get a large, hale, hearty Negro man from some other plantation to go to his Negro woman. He would ask the other master to let this man come over to his place to go to his slave girls. A slave girl was expected to have children as soon as she became a woman. Some of them had children at the age of twelve and thirteen years old. Negro men six feet tall went to some of these children.[20]

Many Black females were bought and sold based on their reproductive potential. As Willie Coffer recalls, "A good young breedin' 'oman brung two thousand dollars easy, 'cause all de marsters wanted to see plenty of strong healthy chillun comin' on, all de time."[21] Most damaging to the Black woman's reputation were articles that appeared discussing her reproductive capacity. These articles would speculate on the best conditions for the proper breeding of slaves. They also marveled at the fertility of enslaved women. Reinforcing this "breeder" mystique was the fact that enslaved women were often forced back into the fields only days, sometimes hours, after delivering. They were also expected to get pregnant as often as possible. Deborah Gray White poignantly captures the Black females' dilemma, "Once [enslaved women's] reproduction became a topic of public conversation, so did the slave woman's sexual activities. People accustomed to speaking and writing about the bondwoman's reproductive abilities could hardly help associating her with licentious behavior."[22]

Black women were helplessly trapped in the mythology of being Jezebels by the very institution that demanded them to be precisely that. The more entrenched the Jezebel image became, the easier it was to justify treating Black women in inhumane ways. Once enslaved females were considered Jezebels, then all manner of treatment of them was deemed appropriate. They could be worked brutally in the fields, displayed on public auction blocks like cattle, and exploited as breeders.

Adding to the persistence of the Jezebel imagery was the fact that this image was necessary to ideas of White male and female privilege and superiority. The Black woman as a Jezebel was a perfect foil to the White, middle-class woman who was pure, chaste, and innocent. As White notes: "In every way Jezebel was the counterimage of the mid-nineteenth-century ideal of the Victorian lady. She did not lead men and children to God; piety was foreign to her. She saw no advantage in prudery, indeed domesticity paled in importance before matters of the flesh."[23]

One of the practical consequences of this counterimage was that it allowed White men to sexually exploit Black women while still protecting the innocence of White women. Black women served as a buffer. They were the unwilling recipients of the most depraved passions of White husbands, fathers, and sons. As the daughter of a former slave said, "out of sight of their own women . . . , men in high position, whose wives and daughters [were] leaders of society," preyed on Black women.[24] Leon Litwack clarifies the hypocrisy of White men as he notes: "[E]ven as white men venerated their women as the repositories of virtue and purity, some of them saw no contradiction in violating the bodies and minds of black women, in keeping black mistresses, and in patronizing black-run houses of prostitution."[25]

Essentially, Black women were ensnared in a system that labeled them Jezebels and then compelled them into a "promiscuous" life. As formerly enslaved Madison Jefferson recalled, "Women who refuse to submit themselves to the brutal desires of their owners, are repeatedly whipt to subdue their virtuous repugnance, and in most instances this hellish practice is but too successful."[26] The depth of the degradation and humiliation of the Jezebel trap is recalled in another slave testimony:

Oh, how often I've seen the poor girls sob and cry, when there's been such goings on! Maybe you think, because they're slaves, they an't got no feeling and no shame? A woman's being a slave, don't stop her having genteel ideas; that is, according to their way, and as far as they can. They know they must submit to their masters; besides, their masters maybe, dress'em up and make'em little presents, and give'em more privileges, while the whim lasts; but that an't like having a parcel of low, dirty, swearing, drunk patter-rollers let loose among'em, like so many hogs. This breaks down their spirits dreadfully, and makes 'em wish they was dead.[27]

Also made clear from the slaves' stories is the fact that White molesters were not held accountable for their misdeeds or responsible for any offspring that may have resulted from their sexual rampages. These White male rapists justified their defilement of Black females by claiming that the women asked for it: they (the Jezebels that they were) were the seducers. The children from these violent encounters would, therefore, never become a real threat to the purity of the White race. While such children certainly disturbed the "happiness" of many a White household and were a source of anguish for many a White wife, White men were not obliged to recognize or support them. Again, the responsibility and blame for the sexual encounters belonged to the Black woman. The White man was considered a victim of an evil seduction and was thus not responsible for whatever came from such seductive machinations. To ensure White male impunity on this matter, laws were quickly passed throughout the South that followed the principle that children follow in the condition of their mothers. With laws such as these, there was little danger that children resulting from White men's rape of enslaved women would be considered anything more than slaves. They certainly would not be accepted into the mainstream of White family or social life. As Deborah Gray White points out, "The image of Jezebel excused miscegenation, the sexual exploitation of black women, and the mulatto population."[28]

By distorting Black women's sexuality, the Jezebel image protected the White slavocracy and fostered the exercise of tyrannical White power. Yet as significant as the Jezebel image was to the slavocracy and White power in general, it was effective only inasmuch as it functioned in conjunction with another powerful and tenacious image foisted upon Black women — that of Mammy.

Mammy

It would not do in the White, racist, patriarchal world of slavery for Black women to be *only* Jezebels. White households could not be entrusted to the care of Jezebels. Such morally reprehensible creatures were certain to damage the moral upbringing of White children and to be an improper influence upon innocent White women. Moreover, if all Black women were Jezebels, then White men would be truly overwhelmed by the presence of so many seductive creatures. The "gentility" of the southern slavocracy demanded the image of Mammy. As historian Patricia Morton observes, "the more [the Black woman] was treated and viewed as a Jezebel, the more essential Mammy became as the counterimage of slavery's racial imagery."[29] This image served to "calm Southern fears of moral slippage and 'mongrelization,' or man's fears of woman's emasculating sexual powers."[30] But who, exactly, was Mammy?

While southern lore paints Mammy as the perfect female slave, obedient and completely loyal to the master's family, sometimes even to the point of being disloyal to other enslaved people, the reality of Mammy is more ambiguous. Testimony suggests a much more complex figure.

If Mammy was a trustful caretaker of her master's and mistress's children, it was not at the expense of her own children's care. She oftentimes found a way to take care of both, even when her slaveholders demanded total devotion to their own children. Typically, Mammy was an older female and thus conformed to the image of being maternal and asexual. Yet she was sometimes young and attractive, thus frequently victimized by the White males of the household. Sometimes Mammy may have been a trusted confidante of the White mistress. But oftentimes she was perceived as a sexual threat and was the victim of her mistress's violent tirades. If her duties as domestic servant were less strenuous than those of a fieldhand, being in the master's house meant that she was on twenty-four-hour call. If, as a domestic servant, Mammy received better clothing and more food, being in the master's house also meant she was more subject to his whims of violence, sexual or otherwise. So if Mammy appeared docile and subservient, it may have been only a ruse for surviving when living in such close quarters with the master and mistress. If Mammy was a trusted confidante of the mistress, she was also a friend on the inside for the other enslaved persons. James Curry, who himself had been enslaved, offers a compelling portrait of his mother's life as Mammy:

My mother was cook in the house for about twenty-two years. She cooked for from twenty-five to thirty-five, taking the family and the slaves together. . . . After my mistress's death, my mother was the only woman kept in the house. She took care of my master's children, some of whom were then quite small, and brought them up. . . . After she had raised my master's children, one of his daughters, a young girl, came into the kitchen one day, and for some trifle about the dinner, she struck my mother, who pushed her away, and she fell on the floor. Her father was not at home. When he came home . . . [the girl] told him about it. He came down, called my mother out, and, with a hickory rod, he beat her fifteen or twenty strokes, and then called his daughter and told her to take her satisfaction of her, and she did beat her until she was satisfied. . . . My mother's labor was very hard. She would go to the house in the morning, take her pail upon her head, and go away to the cow-pen, and milk fourteen cows. She then put on the bread for the family breakfast. . . . After clearing away the family breakfast, she got breakfast for the slaves. . . . In the meantime, she had beds to make, rooms to sweep. . . . Then she cooked the family dinner. . . . At night she had the cows to milk again. . . . This was her work day by day. Then in the course of the week, she had the washing and ironing to do for her master's family . . . and for her husband, seven children and herself.[31]

Notwithstanding the vivid picture that Curry provides of his mother's life as Mammy/household servant, there are those who also claim that the idea of a Mammy, a trusted female servant, is more fiction than fact. Historian Catherine Clinton argues:

This familiar denizen [Mammy] of the Big House is not merely a stereotype, but in fact a figment of the combined romantic imaginations of the contemporary southern ideologue and the modern southern historian. Records do acknowledge the presence of female slaves who served as the "right hand" of plantation mistresses. Yet documents from the planter class during the first fifty years following the American Revolution reveal only a handful of such examples. Not until after Emancipation did black women run white households or occupy in any significant number the special positions ascribed to them in folklore and fiction. The Mammy was created by white Southerners to redeem the relationship between black women and white men within slave society in response to the antislavery attack from the North during the ante-bellum era, and to embellish it with nostalgia in the post-bellum period. In the primary records from before the Civil War, hard evidence for its existence simply does not appear.[32]

Clearly Mammy is one of the more complex and elusive figures of enslavement. That there were Black female house servants is indisputable. The prevalence of them and the nature of their work are more difficult to determine. There is simply not a single picture that can be painted of the life or labor of the enslaved female domestic. Yet while the actual role and life of these women may be unclear, the significance of the Mammy image to White, racist, patriarchal culture is most clear. Whether the "perfect" Mammy existed in the minds of the slavocracy or was real is less significant than how this role — the household female servant/Mammy — preserved White female and male prestige and privilege.

By acting as a surrogate mother, Mammy allowed White women to maintain their Victorian role as perfect mothers. While White women may have handed down certain moral and religious values to their children, Mammy performed the more mundane and physical tasks of rearing children, even to the point of nursing White infants. Despite being labeled asexual, Mammy still performed the kind of functions that reflected Black women's so-called sensual nature. Barbara Christian astutely explains:

> All the functions of mammy are magnificently physical. They involve the body as sensuous, as funky, the part of woman that white southern America was profoundly afraid of. Mammy, then, harmless in her position of slave, unable because of her all-giving nature to do harm, is needed as an image, a surrogate to contain all those fears of the physical female.[33]

Patricia Hill Collins expands:

> "Good" white mothers are expected to deny their female sexuality and devote their attention to the moral development of their offspring. In contrast, the mammy image is one of an asexual woman, a surrogate mother in blackface devoted to the development of a white family.[34]

Notwithstanding Mammy's importance to reinforcing the role of woman as perfect mother, Mammy was most notable as an alternative to the Jezebel image. For its own survival, the White patriarchal slavocracy needed White culture to portray a convincing image of an enslaved female that was more domesticated than Jezebel. Mammy was the answer. For some, she symbolized the "civilizing" potential of slavery. (In this regard Mammy was the female counterpart to the Black male "Sambo" image, as they were both portrayed as happy, docile, domesticated slaves.) This image pointed to the opportunity slavery provided for training and uplifting Black women. Mammy meant that it was possible for Black women to become something other than Jezebels. The logic of White culture implied that with the help of slavery Black women could actually come close — through their care of White children — to personifying the Victorian image of women as happy homemakers.

Mammy symbolized both the perfect female and the perfect slave. She was the happy homemaker, the rearer of White children, and the dutifully obedient slave to her master and mistress. Deborah Gray White offers one of the most comprehensive summaries of Mammy's import to White hegemony:

> Mammy was, thus, the perfect image for antebellum Southerners. As the personification of the ideal slave, and the ideal woman, Mammy was an ideal symbol of the patriarchal tradition. She was not just a product of the "cultural uplift" theory, she was *also* a product of the forces that in the South raised motherhood to sainthood. As a part of the benign slave tradition, and as a part of the cult of domesticity, Mammy was the centerpiece in the antebellum Southerner's perception of the perfectly organized society....
>
> Mammy symbolized race and sex relations at their best. She was at once black and female. In reality, as well as in mythology, both blacks and women were ultimately subservient to white males.[35]

The significance of Jezebel and Mammy to the institution of slavery, and more especially to White patriarchal power, shows why these images are so central to White culture and thus so persistent and abiding. By distorting the sexuality of Black women, White culture effectively dehumanized them. Such dehumanization made them most vulnerable to rape by White men. The weapon of rape provided an effective means of control. In essence, the Jezebel and Mammy images crafted in White culture allowed White people to cruelly exploit Black female bodies with relative impunity. Such exploitation is a linchpin to the survival of White hegemony. For this reason, these stereotypic images have endured and even, as we shall see later, reappear in various forms in contemporary society.

VIOLENT BUCKS

These images of Black womanhood provided a gateway to the dehumanization of Black men. The Jezebel character in particular has provided an excuse for the sexual degradation of these males. That Black women were considered sexual reprobates provided White culture with the fundamental proof of the inevitable nature of Black men's sexual perversion. That Black women were Jezebels meant that Black men had no choice but to be passionate and lascivious, if for no other reason than to fulfill the sexual desires of the "hot" Black woman. One southern female writer put it bluntly in a popular nineteenth-century periodical: "They [black women] are evidently the chief instruments of the degradation of the men of their race."[36] In order to complement the unrestrained Black woman, White culture portrayed Black men as wild, bestial, violent bucks.

Black men were regarded, like their female counterparts, as highly sexualized, passionate beings. They were considered lewd, lascivious, and also quite sexually proficient. Black male sexual prowess has become almost legend in the stereotypic logic of White culture. The idea that Black men possess an unusually large penis has only reinforced notions of their sexual aggressiveness and mastery. According to Winthrop Jordan, the ideas about Black male genitalia predate the settlement of America and possibly even the Portuguese explorations of the West African coast. To be sure, Jordan says, "By the final quarter of the eighteenth century the idea that the Negro's penis was larger than the white man's had become something of a commonplace in European scientific circles."[37] Exemplifying the persistence of these myths, novelist Richard Wright remembered a time when two White employees questioned the size of his penis, goading him to "spin around on it like a top."[38] These beliefs surrounding the Black man's sexual temperament and physical attributes no doubt contributed to the White cultural image of the Black man as a buck.

As a buck, the enslaved male was quite useful to the slavocracy. He was deemed a powerful animal not only in terms of his abilities to produce work, but also in terms of his ability to breed offspring. Yet, as indispensable as this image of the Black buck was to the institution of slavery, it also posed a potential threat to the peace and sanctity of the White world. For if being a Jezebel meant that Black women were seducers, then being a buck meant that Black men were sexual predators. Even more threatening to White existence was the idea that the common prey of bucks was White women. Having painted Black women in such a vile manner, White culture then had to accept the notion that these women would not be attractive even to their own men. As is so aptly explained by Paula Giddings (using the words of Philip A. Bruce, a nineteenth-century Virginia aristocrat and historian known for his White supremacist views), the discomfiting logic of White culture suggested that "it was the white women's qualities, so profoundly missing in black women, that made black men find white women irresistible and 'strangely alluring and seductive.'"[39] One Black man eloquently refuted this notion, however, by pointing the finger back at the White man. In an 1866 Emancipation Day speech, Henry Turner said: "We have as much beauty as they; *all we ask of the white man is to let our ladies alone*, and they need not fear us. The difficulty has heretofore been *our ladies were not always at our disposal.*"[40]

Finally, the "wisdom" of White culture advised that a passionate, unrestrained Black buck was also by nature feral. This meant that the Black buck posed a danger to the very lives of White men and women.

White culture seemed trapped by its own insidiously racist logic. The Jezebel was not a desired sexual partner for the Black buck, so he was compelled toward White women. The superpotency and virility of the Black male might also mean that White women were erotically attracted to him. It certainly indicated that the Black male was governed by passion and was thus naturally violent. Ironically, this portrait of the Black buck challenged what it was contrived to protect — the notion of White male superiority. The buck imposed upon White women, impugned White manhood, and threatened White lives. Manning Marable best describes the threat of the Black male to White patriarchal society:

> [White males'] point of view of Black males was conditioned by three basic beliefs. Black men were only a step above the animals — possessing awesome physical power but lacking in intellectual ability.... Second, the Black male represented a potential political threat to the entire system of slavery. And third, but by no means last, the Black male symbolized a lusty sexual potency that threatened white women.... Another dilemma, seldom

discussed publicly, was the historical fact that some white women of all social classes were not reluctant to request the sexual favors of their male slaves.[41]

Castration

Yet, despite the implied power of the Black buck, White culture was relentless in its portrayal. Instead of reconfiguring the images painted of Black people to escape the inevitable conclusions of racist logic, it sanctioned the tools necessary to keep the virile, fiery Black man in his place. Black male bodies were attacked and dismembered with impunity. Castration, though objected to by some Englishmen and abolitionists, became a punishment meted out to Black men. It was initially used as a penalty for running away, plotting insurrection, or similar offenses in the eyes of the slaveholding class. With continued outcry from abolitionists and others about its practice, by the eighteenth century it became a punishment primarily in accusations of rape. By definition rape could only happen to White women. No such crime as rape of a Black woman existed. Such a crime would be ludicrous since Black women "were said to give themselves willingly, even wantonly, to white men."[42] Yet slave-masters often castrated those enslaved males whom they believed to be barriers to their own vile desires to ravish a particular Black woman. Jordan describes the sinister motives behind castration:

> Castration of Negroes clearly indicated a desperate, generalized need in white men to persuade themselves that they were really masters and in all ways masterful, and it illustrated dramatically the ease with which white men slipped over into treating their Negroes like their bulls and stallions whose "spirit" could be subdued by emasculation. In some colonies, moreover, the specifically sexual aspect of castration was so obvious as to underline how much of the White man's insecurity vis-à-vis the Negro was fundamentally sexual.[43]

Lynching

As odious as castration was, no crime against the Black man more clearly indicated the White male fear of Black male sexuality or power than lynching. The phenomenon of lynching clearly exemplifies Foucault's understanding of the relationship between sexual discourse and the exercise of power. Through careful deployment of discourse about Black male sexuality, White society was able to easily embrace lynching

as a necessary means for protection against such a passionate animal.
Leon Litwack explains:

> To endorse lynching was to dwell on the sexual depravity of
> blacks, to raise the specter of the black beast seized by uncontrol-
> lable savage sexual passions that were inherent in the race. That
> is, the inhumanity, depravity, bestiality, and savagery practiced by
> white participants in lynchings would be justified in the name of
> humanity, morality, justice, civilization, and Christianity.[44]

Even as lynching was clearly a sexually directed and motivated attack against Black male bodies, it was a primary weapon employed to
control Black men and women socially, economically, and politically.
Lynching is thus a classic example of the tools used to enforce and
uphold White patriarchal hegemony. Lynching rose in popularity after
emancipation. With the nominal end of slavery, there was no clear way
to control the movement or perceived threat of thousands of once enslaved people turned loose on White society. In an effort to maintain
control, White society made certain that the old stereotypes that supported the slavocracy would continue in effect. Black women remained
vulnerable to rape — as they were still thought of as little more than
Jezebels. Herbert Gutman describes the plight of the emancipated female this way: "Ex-slave women everywhere dealt with a legacy that
viewed them as dependent sexual objects."[45] White poignantly comments: "Black women continued to be perceived by white America as
individuals who desired promiscuous relationships, and this perception
left them vulnerable to sexual crimes.... As far as the Jezebel image was
concerned, the Thirteenth Amendment freed no black woman."[46]

If the Black woman was most vulnerable to rape, the emancipated
male — still thought of as a violent buck — was vulnerable to being
lynched. Indeed, almost three thousand Black people were reportedly
lynched between 1889 and 1918. Some fifty were women, and thus
the overwhelming number were Black men. While lynchings were justified by the claim that the man hanged had violated a White woman,
it was more often simply "rumors of rape" that led to such lynchings.
The real threat to White male supremacy probably rested in the knowledge that some White women were actually attracted to Black men
and voluntarily entered into a relationship with them. As Gutman has
shown, "There is also scattered evidence indicating sexual contact and
even marital connections between southern white women and slave
and ex-slave men."[47] Ida B. Wells bluntly states, "White men lynch

the offending Afro-American not because he is a despoiler of virtue, but because he succumbs to the smiles of white women."[48] Again, it would seem that the discourse surrounding the Black man's virility was so effective that it backfired in terms of protecting the purity of White women and hence of the White race.

But, again, the perceived threat to White male supremacy went beyond Black men's real or imagined sexual contact with White women. Lynching was not simply utilized as a remedy for an imagined sexual crime; it was a response to social, political, and economic challenges that White men felt from Black males. Essentially, it was a reaction to a perceived threat to White supremacy. Litwack puts the matter plainly: "Victims of lynch mobs, more often than not, had challenged or unintentionally violated the prevailing norms of white supremacy, and these ranged from the serious offenses (in the eyes of whites) to the trivial."[49]

Stories such as that of the Black Florida town of Rosewood illustrate the true motivation of lynch mobs. In 1932 some one hundred Black men, women, and children lost their lives as the town was destroyed by White mobs. Black men were lynched and castrated. Black women were raped and lynched. After all was said and done, scores of Black people were dismembered and killed during this violent rampage. The reign of White terror ostensibly began over a rumor of rape of a White woman by a Black man. While the rape or even the rumor of rape may be disputed as the reason for the White terror, it is most clear that the real reason for the crimes against Black people in Rosewood had to do with White resentment over the very existence of a Black town, with prospering Black men and women who lived relatively free from White rule and power.

The story of Ida B. Wells's entrance into the battle against lynching also reveals the impetus of lynching. Ms. Wells began her courageous campaign to end lynching after her friend Thomas Moss was lynched on March 9, 1892, for the "crime" of owning a successful grocery store that rivaled the success of a White grocery. With the support of sexual discourse, lynching became an effective way to prevent Black people from gaining power politically, economically, or socially. As Ida B. Wells knew well, "lynching and the rape of black women were attempts to regain control [of black people after emancipation]. The terrorizing of black communities was a political weapon that manipulated ideologies of sexuality."[50]

The terror of rape, castration, and lynching as well as the caricatures that fueled this terror provide incontrovertible evidence of how

Black people's sexuality has been a pawn in White culture's efforts to secure White patriarchal hegemony in American society. The abuse and defilement of Black sexuality are embedded in the very core of White culture. They are as natural to White culture as the very air we breathe. As long as White culture exists, attacks upon Black sexuality will persist. This point is made poignantly clear by the continued presence of the most salient sexual stereotypes.

THE CONTINUED ATTACK ON BLACK SEXUALITY

Jezebel, Mammy, and the Black buck have come full circle. They have been transformed into more contemporary figures. Mammy has become the domineering matriarch. The Jezebel image remains virtually intact and has been carried forth in the portrayal of Black women as welfare mothers/queens. Like Jezebel, the Black male continues to suffer from being cast as beastly. Let us now explore these contemporary portraits.

Mammy to Matriarch: The Moynihan Report

The portrait of Black women as Mammy lasted long after slavery largely because the jobs most available to Black women have been as domestic workers in White households. Deborah Gray White intuits, "Surely there is some connection between the idea of Mammy, the service and domestic jobs readily offered to black women, and their near-exclusion from other kinds of work."[51] As a Mammy or domestic worker, Black women were exploited for the economic advantage of White society. While Mammy provided free labor, the grossly underpaid domestic worker provided cheap labor. Like Mammy, these Black domestic workers cared for the house and reared the White children. However, as domestic workers Black women performed the mundane duties of White motherhood that allowed White women to take their places not on Victorian pedestals, but with White men in the workplace.

If during slavery Mammy was sometimes criticized for neglecting her own children, as a domestic worker she was castigated for providing for her family. The movement from Mammy to domestic worker placed the Black woman in a double bind that led to her being considered a domineering matriarch. Patricia Hill Collins explains:

> Mammy [meaning a domestic worker] is the ideal Black mother for she recognizes her place. She is paid next to nothing yet cheerfully accepts her inferior status. But when she enters her own

home, this same Mammy is transformed into the second image, the too-strong matriarch who raises weak sons and "unnaturally superior" daughters.[52]

The idea of the Black woman as a powerful matriarch, most commonly referred to in stereotypic language as Sapphire, was cemented in White culture by a 1965 report on the "Negro family" by Daniel P. Moynihan, who at the time was assistant secretary of labor and director of the Office of Policy Planning and Research in the Johnson administration.[53] The report opens by presenting the "deterioration of the Negro family" as the "fundamental source of the weakness of the Negro community." It goes on to argue that the Negro family is at the heart of a "tangle of pathology" that perpetuates poverty and antisocial behavior within the Black community. Essentially, Moynihan identified family "disorganization" as the major source of weakness for the Black community. In so doing, he clearly named the Black woman as the culprit. She was considered the root cause for the "tangle of pathology" that ensnared the Black family. She, Moynihan argued, was the center of a "black matriarchy" that was the core of the problem, imposing "a crushing burden on the Negro male."

It is important to note at this point the significance of the Black family to the White cultural attack upon Black sexuality. If the family is the source of communicating values and ways of behaving to a people, then to suggest a "deviant" family is to imply the handing down of deviant values and standards. To stigmatize the family is to stigmatize the entire race of people. Paul Gilroy explains, "The family is not just the site of cultural reproduction; it is also identified as the mechanism for reproducing the cultural dysfunction that disables the race as a whole."[54] The Moynihan Report therefore perpetuated the perception of Black people as deviant, especially as Moynihan attacked the Black family by means of Black sexuality.

Because Black women could often find work while Black men could not, the Moynihan Report blamed Black women for depriving Black men of their masculine right to provide for their families and, as he said, "to strut" like a "bantam rooster" or "four star general." By blaming Black women for the plight of Black men and hence the plight of the Black family, the report directed attention away from the social, economic, and political structures — all of them racist and patriarchal — that actually deprived Black men of work and relegated Black women to domestic labor.

The Moynihan Report also strongly implied that Black women were responsible for the failure of Black children to achieve. According to Moynihan, Black boys in female-led homes were in particular jeopardy. Lacking strong Black male role models, the boys were destined to be sexually confused, to demonstrate various antisocial behaviors, and to become welfare dependent. The overall effect was that Black families would remain in poverty, because Black men would be so emasculated by Black women that they would never be able to contribute to the uplift and economic well-being of Black families. Moreover, Black children, especially boys, would not acquire the skills for climbing out of the poverty cycle. In actuality, the Moynihan Report perpetuated the myth that "the crisis of black politics and social life [is] a crisis solely of black masculinity.... It is to be repaired by instituting appropriate forms of masculinity and male authority, intervening in the family to rebuild the race."[55]

The ultimate coup of the Moynihan Report, however, was the way it shrewdly manipulated Black female sexuality. Moynihan shamelessly identified "Black women's failure to conform to the cult of true womanhood...as one fundamental source of Black cultural deficiency."[56] If Mammy in the White home is a de-sexed figure, then Mammy as matriarch in the Black home is an oversexed figure. "The matriarch represents the sexually aggressive woman, one who emasculates Black men because she will not permit them to assume roles as Black patriarchs."[57]

By skillfully transforming the image of Mammy into that of matriarch, White culture has continued to demean Black women and disparage their sexuality to make it appear that White male hegemony is natural and normal, if not inevitable. The "overachieving" Black woman becomes the scapegoat for the so-called emasculation of Black men. Such emasculation is seen as the basis for these men's lack of success in the social, political, and economic marketplace. In the reasoning of White culture, it is because of the Black matriarch that Black men are unable to exercise political, economic, or social power, and thus the Black community fails to thrive. Audre Lorde clarifies the issue: "[T]he myth of the Black matriarchy as a social disease was presented by racist forces to redirect our attentions away from the real sources of Black oppression."[58]

Jezebel to Welfare Queen

If the slavocracy's Mammy became contemporary society's matriarch, then Jezebel became the foundation for the idea of the Black woman as a welfare mother/queen. The Black welfare mother/queen is portrayed as one who, like Jezebel, is most suited for breeding children. Welfare mothers are characterized as promiscuous unmarried women who sit around, collect government checks, and give birth to a lot of children. While the offspring of the Jezebels were beneficial to the economy, the offspring of the welfare mothers are seen as detrimental. Therefore, just as White society attempted to regulate the reproductive capacity of enslaved woman, it too has attempted to intervene in the reproductive capacities of the welfare mother. Collins observes, "The image of the welfare mother thus provides ideological justification for the dominant group's interest in limiting the fertility of Black mothers who are seen as producing too many economically unproductive children."[59] Most significantly, however, the Black woman as welfare mother remains essential to White hegemony because the White culture blames the woman for her impoverished condition and again deflects attention away from White, racist, patriarchal structures. In essence, the welfare mother "represents a woman of low morals and uncontrolled sexuality, factors identified as the cause of her impoverished state."[60]

That the welfare mother/queen image continues to be an effective means for seizing and maintaining power in a racist, patriarchal society is illustrated by Supreme Court Justice Clarence Thomas's quest for power. While still a congressional aide, Thomas shamelessly attacked the character of his sister, Emma Mae Martin. In front of a 1980 San Francisco conference sponsored by Black Republicans, he depicted Ms. Martin as a quintessential welfare queen. He painted a false picture of her as the stereotypic Black breeder woman who shirks responsibilities for her children by going on welfare and consequently models this slothful behavior to her sons and daughters. He announced to laughter that his sister "gets mad when the mailman is late with her welfare check. That's how dependent she is. What's worse is that now her kids feel entitled to the check, too. They have no motivation for doing better or for getting out of that situation."[61]

In his portrayal, Thomas unwittingly disclosed more about himself than about his sister. He revealed that he had been so indoctrinated by White culture that he shared the contempt of Black women found in that culture. Reflective of White cultural animus, he grossly and crudely distorted the truth and maligned a Black woman (his own sister), attacking her character through her sexuality, as a means to support his place in White patriarchal hegemony. His sister became for him a perfect foil to his "meteoric ride" out of the poverty of Pinpoint, Georgia.

As harmful as the Jezebel image has been in its contribution to the image of the Black woman as welfare mother/queen, it has affected Black women even more directly. Black women, even today, are thought of as Jezebels. As Nell Painter has astutely pointed out, "The oversexed-black-Jezebel is more likely than not still taken at face value."[62] This fact was made personally clear to me during my sophomore year at Denison University. It happened one early spring evening when my Black female roommate and I were returning from selecting our dorm room for the next school year. As we entered one of the residential quadrangles, we noticed a crowd of excited White students in a circle who were obviously being entertained by something in the center. We both walked over to see what was causing such uproarious behavior. When we looked into the center of the circle, we were shocked and horrified by what we saw. One of the fraternities was conducting one of its rites of spring by enacting a drama. Central to this drama was a White male in blackface, costumed as an African woman (with a grass skirt and spear in hand), prancing around the circle in a stereotypic, tribal-like fashion. As I stood in pained shock, I heard shouted words, "Hey, get down, you African wench." The words deepened the pain, while also making crystal clear to me that I as a Black woman was nothing more than a "wench," a Jezebel to many on that campus. The wider significance of that incident became clear to me only after I left Denison. I later understood that as long as there was a White patriarchal hegemony in America, so fervently protected by White culture, Black women — regardless of our successes — would forever be branded as Jezebels.

The Thomas/Hill Hearings

There is no more poignant example of the continuing power of the Jezebel image than Anita Hill's treatment when she brought charges of sexual harassment against the then-nominee to the Supreme Court, Clarence Thomas. While these hearings were rife with racially and sexually loaded clichés and conventions — some carelessly and selfishly introduced by Thomas himself — none stood out more than those surrounding Anita Hill. Specifically, Anita Hill was portrayed at once as the traitor to and Jezebel of Black men. Thomas employed the trope of the Black female race-traitor effectively in his defense against harassment charges as he argued that he did not know why Hill would want to bring him down in such a fashion. At one point in the proceedings he referred to Hill as "possibly his enemy."[63] At another time during questioning Thomas likened Hill to a family member who betrays another family member.[64]

While Thomas did not dwell on the portrait of Hill as a "traitor," he said just enough to put it on the minds of those who needed a way to discredit Hill. For instance, sympathetic to Thomas's plight as a victim of betrayal, Senator Orrin Hatch said, "We are going to talk a little bit more . . . about how this could have happened. How one person's uncorroborated allegations, could destroy a career and one of the most wonderful opportunities for a young man from Pinpoint, Georgia."[65] Later during the hearings, under the guise of seeking understanding, Hatch would approvingly quote a Black man who said, "She [Hill] is trying to demonize us [Black men]."[66]

As encumbered as Hill may have been with the trope of a Black female race-traitor, the Black woman as Jezebel was perhaps the most difficult myth for her to escape. Thomas portrayed her as a vengeful woman whose flirtations were spurned, and as one who was angry because of his interest in lighter complexioned (that is, White, such as his wife) women. In his defense, witnesses came forward who characterized Hill as a tease who became vindictive in the face of rejection.[67] Even to the surprise of Anita Hill, the all-White male panel allowed for such unmerited portrayals, and some even bought into them. In response to one of Thomas's witnesses who portrayed Hill as a spurned woman who was psychologically impaired, Hill would later say, "The admission of testimony like [John] Dogget's in a proceeding as important as this is hard to believe. The reality of experiencing it, however, was completely appalling."[68]

After all was said and done, Anita Hill's charges of sexual harassment did not stand a chance of ever being taken seriously. Clarence Thomas had successfully masterminded her undoing by providing the bait necessary for others to see Anita Hill as the typical Black Jezebel. Hill, the female, became the villain. Thomas, the male, became the victim. In the scenario carefully orchestrated by Thomas, Hill, the so-called Jezebel, was caught in her own web. This time she was caught seducing a Black man instead of a White man. That she could have been a victim of sexual harassment was thus impossible. A Jezebel, after all, asks for whatever sexual treatment she receives, from harassment to rape. Painter sums up the consequence of the Jezebel influence in the Thomas case when she says:

The belief persists that black women are always ready for sex and, as a consequence, cannot be raped. Introducing the specter of sex, Hill made herself vulnerable to Virginia Thomas's [Clarence's White wife] retort: Hill — as both the oversexed black Jezebel anxious for sex and as the rejected, vindictive woman who trumps up a charge of sexual harassment — really wanted to sleep with Clarence Thomas. The injury, then, is to him, not to her.[69]

The Thomas hearings poignantly illustrate the powerful legacy of the sexual stereotypes crafted during slavery in relation to Black women. They continue to be pertinent in the exercise of White patriarchal power, even when it is a man born Black who is attempting to protect and share in that power. The resolve by which White culture protects White male hegemony renders it virtually impossible for Black women to step out of the character of Jezebel. Likewise, this culture has ensnared Black men in the image of the violent, raping buck.

The Violent Black Man

White culture effectively maintained the image of the Black male as a violent, raping buck long after chattel slavery. The tragedies of Black history are a testament to this fact. As mentioned earlier, "rumors of rape" have consistently led to Black men being lynched and castrated far into the twentieth century. In 1955 while visiting relatives in Mississippi, fourteen-year-old Emmit Till was lynched and mutilated for allegedly whistling at a White woman. As recently as 1989 the Black community in Boston was harshly dealt with after a White man falsely claimed that his pregnant wife was murdered by a Black man. As it turned out, he himself had killed his wife. This fact came to light, however, only after the police infiltrated Black communities, where they brutally harassed and summarily rounded up Black men. Cases such as these have made it crystal clear that the folklore of the African American community is actually true: "A Black man should not be caught dead coming into contact with a White woman." There is no more powerful example of this than the O. J. Simpson case.

Like the Thomas hearings, this case teems with racial and gender stereotypes. It offers a case study on the interplay among sex, race, and power in the United States. The Simpson saga, for instance, immediately calls forth images such as Richard Wright's Bigger Thomas. Ishmael Reed says of the connection between Simpson and the fictional Thomas:

On other occasions, Simpson was compared to Bigger Thomas. On the surface, the two have little in common. . . .

What Bigger and O. J. Simpson do have in common is that both were arrested for the murder of blond white women, both were subjected to a mob-rule public opinion that convicted them before all of the evidence was examined, and both were tried in the media, which, instead of serving as an objective reporter of the facts, inflamed the situation and contributed to a racial divide.[70]

From out of the cacophony of messages that White America was sending to Black America through the almost perverse media attention given to this case, one stood out. Black men be warned: the White male world of power and White women is absolutely off-limits. You will pay the price for entering this world.

Ironically, prior to the media spectacle made of the O. J. Simpson saga, Simpson had successfully navigated the White world of glamour and power, to the point of virtually abandoning the Black world. Yet the moment he was suspected of killing a White woman, the White world of which he considered himself so much a part turned against him. It quickly reminded him that he was Black, even if he had been forgetting this fact. For instance, the June 27, 1994, *Time* magazine cover was a darkened illustration of Simpson. Simpson's image on the cover was reminiscent of the photo of the Black rapist Willie Horton used in the 1988 presidential campaign. Both images were meant to send a visceral message: Black men (that includes O. J. Simpson) are nothing more than violent, raping brutes. The *Time* cover also profoundly signaled that the Simpson case would be about race. Law professor and legal analyst Kimberle Williams Crenshaw explains:

Nowhere was Simpson's symbolic "return" to his essential blackness more graphically illustrated and debated than in the *Time* magazine cover that darkened his face. Many African Americans saw in the illustration proof of their suspicions that race would certainly shape public discourse around the case. Even whites who steadfastly denied that race would have anything to do with the case were troubled by *Time*'s cover illustration.[71]

The media and prosecution nurtured the image of Simpson as a violent brute when they painstakingly depicted him as one whose passion and jealously threw him into a violent rage that resulted in the brutal

slaying of his ex-wife and her male friend. The media spectacle, the un-
natural interest White men and women had in the case, as well as the
trial and civil retrial, made one thing clear: no Black man will get away
with defiling a White woman. It was bad enough that Simpson flaunted
his intimate relationships with these women, but to abuse and kill one
was absolutely intolerable.

When all was said and done, the Simpson case was not about one
man's guilt or innocence. There is little doubt that the case would have
taken on an entirely different tone had it not involved a high-profile
Black man accused of killing a blonde, blue-eyed *White* woman. The
Simpson judicial/media fiasco was about nothing less than the sexual
politics of White hegemony in America. With Simpson as its pawn,
White culture sought to confirm its notion that Black males pose a
severe threat to the sanctity of the White world. The Simpson hype was
about making clear that Black men — regardless of how domesticated
they may appear (meaning assimilated in the White world) — are still
nothing more than violent, passionate beasts of prey. Given this fact,
in the Simpson case White culture used all of its tools to show that
Black men *will not* get away with challenging White male superiority,
especially when that challenge involves the defilement of White female
purity. Toni Morrison says it best:

> Like *Birth of a Nation* the [Simpson] case has generated a newer,
> more sophisticated national narrative of racial supremacy. But
> it is still the old sham white supremacy forever wedded to and
> dependent upon faux black inferiority....
>
> The official story has thrown Mr. Simpson into [a] represen-
> tative role. He is not an individual who underwent and was
> acquitted from a murder trial. He has become the whole race
> needing correction, incarceration, censoring, silencing; the race
> that needs its civil rights disassembled; the race that is sign and
> symbol of domestic violence; the race that has made the trial by
> jury a luxury rather than a right and placed affirmative action
> legislation in even greater jeopardy. This is the consequence and
> function of official stories: to impose the will of a dominant cul-
> ture. It is *Birth of a Nation* writ large — menacingly and pointedly
> for the 'hood.[72]

From the Clarence Thomas hearings to the Simpson saga, it is obvious that the myths and stereotypes surrounding Black people's sexuality
are still prevalent. Mammy, Jezebel, and the violent buck remain es-

sential to White culture's defense of White hegemony. They effectively serve their purpose as stereotypes. They deflect attention from the sinister nature of White power. Indeed, these assaults on Black sexuality make it appear that White supremacy is "natural and inevitable," given the intrinsic depravity of Black people.

CONCLUSIONS

Through the exploration of specific stereotypes this chapter has confirmed that the attack on Black people's sexuality is intrinsic to White culture in its protection of White hegemony. The stereotypes that form the basis of this attack go to the very nature of White culture itself. This is a culture that exists only as it is defined over and against that which is non-White. The images of Black women as Jezebels or Mammies and Black men as violent bucks bolster ideas of White male and female superiority by presenting a picture of Black men and women as inferior. Again, White culture promotes the idea of White supremacy only as this is defined in opposition to that which is non-White.

This study of Black sexual stereotypes has also shown, as suggested by Foucault, that sexual discourse is instrumental in the exercise of power, especially unjust power. In this case, the use of sexual discourse to distort Black people's sexuality as a means of degrading them has been critical to the success of White culture. The startling reality of these findings is that as long as White culture exists, attacks on Black sexuality will also exist in some form. These attacks are as pervasive and enduring as the culture that has given them birth.

The question now to be asked is, What impact has such a sustained and odious attack had upon Black people?

PART 2

THE IMPACT OF THE WHITE CULTURAL ATTACK

CHAPTER 3

The Legacy of White Sexual Assault

Learning to laugh at White culture's guileful derision of Black sexuality is certainly one of the keys to Black sanity in America. Black culture is replete with wit, music, literature, art, and folklore that mockingly relate White culture's conferral of unreasoning zeal and adroitness upon Black people when it comes to their sexual temperament and conduct. The supposed sexual prowess and endowments of Black males are particularly favorite subjects of Black cultural mockery. But while the repartee of Black culture certainly reveals Black people's full cognizance of White cultural stereotypes, as well as their ability to rebuff them, does it belie the full impact of these stereotypes on Black lives? Is the effect of the White cultural attack upon Black bodies and intimacy seen only in the raillery of Black culture? Or has there been a more incisive impact upon the way Black men and women view themselves, one another, and even their God? Has the White cultural attack upon Black people exercised a command over their sexuality so abstruse and penetrating that it foils attempts to grasp and understand its impact? This chapter seeks to answer these questions by exploring how Black people's responses to their own sexuality and related issues have been affected by White culture's incessant animalization of them.

MORE THAN A REFLECTION OF WHITE CULTURE

Before looking at the impact of White culture on Black people, it is important to understand that Black sexuality is not simply a reaction to or a reflection of this destructive culture. It exhibits the copious, manifold mosaic of who Black people are as an African people, constrained to forge a life under death-dealing circumstances.

Black people did not come from Africa as tabulae rasae. They came to America possessing a dynamic culture, an intricate worldview, and delicate patterns of relationships. They utilized this African heritage, though it may have been disrespected in the White world, to carve out a reality and a culture in America that affirmed their humanity. This culture can perhaps best be described as a "culture of resistance."[1] This was a culture crafted by Black people that fostered their struggle for life and wholeness and helped them resist those notions and practices that dismissed their humanity. This fact can be seen in the sexual practices, family lives, and intimate relationships of the enslaved population.

•

Many studies have documented the rich family and community life of the enslaved men and women. These studies debunk the notions of the absent slave family and the resultant pathological legacy. This chapter will not review those studies; rather, it will briefly highlight one aspect of the enslaved's sexuality — their intimate relationships in and outside of marriage — to provide an example of how enslaved Black men and women were able to forge a notion of their sexuality that affirmed their personhood and fostered well-being in the community.

Herbert Gutman rightly points out that "no aspect of slave behavior has been more greatly misunderstood than slave sexual mores and practices."[2] Perhaps as a result of holding the enslaved to European/Euro-American sexual norms, as well as being biased by White cultural stereotypes, some interpreters have considered the enslaved community to be governed by a morally rather loose code of sexual behavior. John D'Emilio and Estelle Freedman, for instance, suggest that the songs sung by Blacks during the postslavery era revealed "a relaxed attitude toward sexual matters, in contrast to the mores of Whites."[3]

In reality, the attitude toward sexual activity that emerged in the enslaved community *was* different from that of Whites, but it was not necessarily morally negligent or indifferent. African sexual customs and mores provided the flexibility needed for Black women and men to adjust from a situation of freedom to a situation where someone else had control over their bodies. Such flexibility, however, did not signal a laxity in moral principles. Instead, it revealed standards that allowed for community and family life within the living quarters of the enslaved.

Sexuality in those quarters functioned differently than it did for the dominant culture. It was characterized not so much as a tool for exercising unjust power, but by the familial, communal, and intimate relationships it nurtured, even under conditions that typically vitiated the possibility of enduring relationships. The actual sexual practices and codes defied ideas of Black people as promiscuous. For example, the enslaved population did not harbor the same "hypocritical" condemnation of sexual activity prior to marriage or for children born outside of wedlock as did White society. The access that White people had to Black bodies during the antebellum period mitigated against such a strict code of morality in relation to sexual matters. If indeed the enslaved Africans had come from cultures that in fact condemned premarital sex or ostracized out-of-wedlock children, then any adjustment to the sexual crimes that accompanied enslavement would not have been possible. Enslaved women, to be sure, would have suffered an almost unbearable existence if they had been castigated by their community because of their vulnerability to White men's sexual perversities.

Reflective of many African cultures from which they came, enslaved women were not ostracized for having engaged in premarital sexual activity or for having children outside of marriage. Neither, of course, were enslaved men. John Blassingame points to the possible African roots of these attitudes in his explanation that in some African cultures premarital sex was institutionalized after the onset of puberty. He further states that children outside of wedlock were not seen as a great calamity; in fact, the calamity was barrenness:

> Because Africans so highly valued children, they could neither conceive of the European concept of celibacy nor, like the European, regard sexual intercourse as dirty, evil, or sinful. Puberty rites in West Africa, for instance, were either preceded or followed by training of the young in their sexual responsibilities. Some societies concluded puberty rites of young girls with defloration.[4]

But while premarital sexual activity was acceptable in some African cultures, these same cultures generally forbade extramarital sex. A similar attitude could be found in the enslaved African community. Promiscuous behavior was neither encouraged nor tolerated among the enslaved population. It was often understood that marriage would follow pregnancy, despite the pressures that enslavement placed on the marriage bond.

The institution of slavery did not respect the sanctity of enslaved marriages. Husbands and wives were regularly sold away from one another, depending upon the needs or whims of their masters. Wives were not protected from the abuse of White men. In fact, many enslaved men vowed never to get married so they would not have to watch as their wives were insulted, raped, and otherwise mistreated.[5] Most often, slavemasters denied enslaved men and women access to legal marriage, although they did require an enslaved couple to get their permission to move into a cabin together.

Notwithstanding the indignities of slavery, the value of marriage was not weakened for the enslaved Africans. In some instances they contrived their own rituals, such as "jumping over a broom," to mark a relationship of marriage. Most often, however, these couples were bound together only by affection. Yet as Robert Staples points out, "These bonds were just as strong, even when there was no legal marriage."[6] Remarkably, the enslaved community's respect for the legality of marriage was not diminished. Such respect is evidenced by the scores of former slaves who sought legal marriage after emancipation. Former slave Henry Bibb makes clear the significance of legal marriage to the enslaved when he says, "There [is] no class of people in the United States who so highly appreciate the legality of marriage as those persons who have been held and treated as property."[7] Essentially, the enslaved's attitude toward marriage illustrates the ability to be flexible in terms of traditional customs and mores and yet to maintain a clear moral code for sexual behavior.

Christianity also played a regulative role in the enslaved's sexual behaviors, especially those of women. Church membership among the enslaved and former enslaved population seemed to imply management of sexual activity. These early Black churches particularly proscribed sexual activity of women. Drawing upon testimony from former slaves, Gutman says that "church *initiation* . . . transformed the sexual behavior of young unmarried black women, publicly bridging the difficult transition from prenuptial sexual freedom to marital fidelity. . . . "[8] These young women were expected to refrain from premarital intercourse after joining the church and were greatly censured and castigated if they did not. When asked if joining the church made a difference in the lives of Black women, one Robert Smalls responded, "Yes, sir, the change is very great — as great as between sun shine and a hail storm. She stops all this promiscuous intercourse with men. The rules of the Church are very strict about it."[9]

The early Black churches seemed to impose a standard of propriety and fidelity in relation to sexual matters; yet those standards reflected a definite gender bias. The literature of the enslaved says very little about the expectations of the male's sexual behavior once he joined the church.

Nevertheless, as suggested by the mores surrounding intimate relationships, a sexual ethic was integral to the culture of resistance forged by the enslaved community. These standards of conduct, while certainly tested and influenced by the White enslaving culture, were not a mirror image of White culture. Neither were they merely a response to stereotypes that suggested Black people were nothing but lascivious, wanton creatures. Due in large part to the African culture they brought with them, Black men and women were able to maintain a sense of their bodies and intimate matters that was relatively unsullied by White cultural degradation. They developed patterns of relating that allowed them to nurture their humanity and, hence, some sense of family and community life, even in the most heartless and barbaric conditions.

THE IMPACT OF WHITE CULTURE
UPON BLACK SEXUALITY

It would be dishonest to suggest that White culture has not impacted Black sexuality. It has, and in a most poignant way. Whether or not this impact could be clearly seen in the enslaved community needs further study. But, to be sure, in the contemporary Black community the jolt of White culture on Black sexuality is clear. The most far-reaching impact has been upon Black sexual discourse. Cornel West describes the reactions of many others when he says that, historically, Black institutions such as families, schools, and churches have refused "to engage one fundamental issue: *black sexuality*. Instead, they [run] from it like the plague. And they obsessively [condemn] those places where black sexuality [is] flaunted: the streets, clubs, and the dance-halls."[10] Paula Giddings points to the impact of White culture in her observation that discourse which includes gender *and* sexuality is "the last taboo" in the Black community.[11] Ethicist Emilie Townes implies such an impact when she notes that the Black community is "sexually repressed," that is, unable to speak honestly about matters of sexuality.[12] These comments signal the greatest blow of the White cultural attack, an attack that has rendered the Black community virtually impotent in its ability to conduct frank, open, and demanding discourse concerning matters of sexuality.

Though the Black community is influenced by the same Victorian and Puritanical morality that has made sexuality — especially as it has been so singularly equated with genitalia — a very difficult topic of discussion for most Americans, the reticence that surrounds sexual discourse in the Black community goes beyond the awkwardness that surrounds such discussions in the wider American society. West, Giddings, and other Black scholars have all noted a unique wariness surrounding Black sexual discourse. One Black church woman put it this way: "For Blacks to discuss sexuality publicly is like eating a watermelon in front of White people. All you do is confirm their images of you."[13] A history of having their sexuality exploited and used as a weapon to support their oppression has discouraged the Black community from freely engaging sexual concerns. That such discourse might only affirm the stereotype that Black people are obsessed with sexual matters no doubt strongly undergirds Black people's reticence to openly confront concerns related to sexuality. Some have even noted that the refusal to engage in public sexual discourse is a form of Black cultural resistance to the corrupting influences of White culture, or a survival strategy against White cultural attacks. West makes this point when he says that "struggling black institutions made a Faustian pact with White America: avoid any substantive engagement with black sexuality and your survival on the margins of American society is, at least, possible."[14]

Whatever the case may be, it is clear that the intrusion of White culture upon Black sexuality has interfered with the Black community's ability, in the main, to freely engage sexual concerns. Giddings aptly notes, "It is [African Americans'] historical experience that has shaped or, perhaps more accurately, misshaped the sex/gender issues and discourse in our community."[15] It is important to note in any case that this "misshaping" of sexual discourse has broad implications for Black people's lives. While silence on sexual matters may have benefits, such silence certainly stifles the Black community's ability to disrupt the command of White culture upon Blacks' sexuality.

A SEXUAL DISCOURSE OF RESISTANCE

Michel Foucault recognizes both the importance of discourse, especially sexual discourse, to the maintenance of power and its potential for being disruptive. He says that discourse "undermines and exposes [power]; it renders it fragile and makes it possible to thwart it."[16] He goes on to suggest that while silence may have its benefits in resisting unjust power, "silence and secrecy are a shelter for power, anchoring its prohibitions."[17] In other words, silence in relation to power can mean consent to that power, while a certain type of discourse can function to dismantle and frustrate it.

It is mandatory that the Black community initiate a comprehensive form of sexual discourse if it is to repel and disrupt the power of White culture in relation to Black bodies, sensuality, and spirituality. This discourse can be seen as a sexual discourse of resistance. It would not be contrived simply as a counterdiscourse to that construed by White culture. It would be proactive rather than merely reactive. It would be an intrinsic element of the Black "culture of resistance." It would be a part of the overall discourse that emerges from Black people's consistent efforts to frustrate and disrupt anything that threatens Black life and wholeness. As such, it would expose the oppressive sexual politics of White culture while fostering positive, life-affirming understandings of Black sexuality. By generating its own independent sexual discourse, the Black community could create a disruptive buffer against the detrimental and insidious discourse of White culture. Given the potential significance of such a discourse for the Black community, let us look a little more closely at the nature of such a discourse of resistance.

A sexual discourse of resistance has two central goals: first, to penetrate the sexual politics of the Black community; and, second, to cultivate a life-enhancing approach to Black sexuality within the Black community. These goals suggest several essential tasks to be carried out by this discourse.

A sexual discourse of resistance will expose the manifold impact White culture has on Black sexuality. It will divulge the numerous and insidious ways in which this culture has caricatured and exploited Black sexuality. For instance, a sexual discourse of resistance might critically examine the influence of White culture on Black self-perceptions, Black relationships, and/or Black spirituality — all aspects of sexuality.

A sexual discourse of resistance will also examine "the sexual rhetoric" of the Black community. This discourse will make clear that while the Black community and its institutions have not engaged in a studied and comprehensive sexual discourse, sexual rhetoric has been consistently present. This rhetoric has been most notable in Black music. The blues tradition — "the most prominent secular genre in early twentieth-century black American music" — characteristically explores sexual themes such as intimate relationships, domestic violence, and homosexuality.[18] The blues was indeed an important postemancipation music form as it allowed emancipated Blacks to give expression to their freedom in ways that the music of slavery (such as work songs or spirituals) did not. The blues permitted Black men and women to sing about sexuality. The ability to express their sexuality, according to Angela Davis, was an important sign of freedom for ex-slaves: "Sexuality...was one of the most tangible domains in which emancipation was acted upon and through which its meanings were expressed. Sovereignty in sexual matters marked an important divide between life during slavery and life after emancipation."[19] In this regard, Davis notes that Black working-class women in particular have utilized the blues "as a privileged site in which [they] were free to assert themselves as sexual beings."[20]

The blues, then, is an "idiom that does not recognize taboos," especially for working-class Black people. Davis points out that "whatever figures into the larger picture for working-class African-American realities — however morally repugnant it may be to the dominant culture or to the black bourgeoisie — is an appropriate subject of blues discourse."[21] Given the sexual rhetoric present within the blues tradition, Davis concludes that it is important "to understand the blues as a form that did allow explicit articulations and explorations of sexual politics."[22] The blues, then, has been an important vehicle for Black sexual expression, allowing Black men and women to tell their stories of love and relationships. As such, the blues should be considered an aesthetic precursor of a sexual discourse of resistance and a central source for such a discourse. While its content concerns matters of Black sexuality, the blues has also been a prominent vehicle for challenging dominant ideologies of racism. In particular, the blues provided working-class Blacks the opportunity to explore themes that the Black bourgeoisie and its institutions often avoided, such as sexuality. This tradition also implies the need to include some form of social-economic analysis to discern the different ways in which class and social status might have shaped Black attitudes toward sexuality.

The blues is not the only musical form in the Black community where sexual rhetoric is prominent. Recently, rap music — reflective of "hip-hop" culture — has provided a vehicle for Black youth in particular to explore many aspects of their lives, including sexuality. Hip-hop culture is born in bleak urban conditions. If the blues is the music of the working class, rap is the music of youth trapped in urban ghettoes. Michael Dyson explains:

At their best, rappers shape the tortuous twists of urban fate into lyrical elegies. They represent lives swallowed by too little love or opportunity. They represent themselves and their peers with aggrandizing anthems that boast of their ingenuity and luck in surviving. The art of "representin'" that is much ballyhooed in hip-hop is the witness of those left to tell the afflicted's story.[23]

Although rap delivers a poignant message concerning a segment of Black life in blighted urban America, it has been heavily castigated for some of its violent imagery and sexual rhetoric. In many instances, rap, especially what has come to be known as "gangsta" rap, has perpetuated a "market-place morality" that "reduces individuals to objects of pleasure."[24] This music is also replete with misogynist and homophobic imagery. As Dyson points out, "There's no doubt that gangsta rap is often sexist and that it reflects a vicious misogyny that has seized our nation with frightening intensity."[25] Yet, regardless of the grave misgivings surrounding rap, this music can be an important resource for a sexual discourse of resistance.

Like the blues, rap provides an understanding of how certain segments of the Black community have expressed their sexuality and have perhaps been impacted by White culture. Rap painfully reveals how marketplace representations surrounding Black sexuality have infiltrated a certain population of Black youth. Dyson puts it this way:

> The link between the vulgar rhetorical traditions expressed in gangsta rap and the economic exploitation that dominates the marketplace is real. The circulation of brutal images of black men as sexual outlaws and black females as "ho's" in many gangsta rap narratives mirrors ancient stereotypes of black sexual identity. Male and female bodies are turned into commodities. Black sexual desire is stripped of redemptive uses in relationships of great affection of love. . . .
>   Gangsta rappers, however, don't merely respond to the values and visions of the marketplace; they help shape them as well.[26]

Rap music also underscores the necessity for a sexual discourse of resistance to include socioeconomic analysis. At the same time, this music indicates the need for a stringent religio-cultural analysis. Such an analysis would highlight those expressions of Black culture, inclusive of its music, that foster Black life and well-being and would disavow those that do not. This analysis, as one aspect of a sexual discourse of resistance, would seek to provide the necessary critical analytic tools to help Black men and women evaluate the life-enhancing value, or lack thereof, of their own attitudes about men, women, intimacy, and relationships. In general, the "in-your-face" manner in which rap music exposes the unhealthy views of sexuality present in many segments of the Black community — and not just the hip-hop reality — signals the urgent need for a sexual discourse of resistance.

Finally, a sexual discourse of resistance must engage Black literature, which becomes another significant resource. Literature has often provided a "safe location" for Black men and women to explore their experiences,[27] and themes surrounding Black sexuality are typically prominent. More will be said about Black literature later.

THE MANDATE FOR A SEXUAL DISCOURSE
OF RESISTANCE

Given the enormity of its tasks as well as its pertinence to the Black community, a sexual discourse of resistance must be carried out at all levels of Black living and in the various arenas in which Black people are struggling for life and wholeness. While no one institution or group of people can bear the entire burden of conducting a sexual discourse of resistance, neither is any institution or group of people exempt from this responsibility. Again, in all places where Black people find themselves trying to make a life — the church, home, schools, fraternal and women's organizations — some form of a sexual discourse of resistance must be carried out. And the complex nature of the discourse requires that various individuals with a range of expertise — social scientists, political scientists, economists, theologians, artists, and others — must contribute even as they enter into dialogue with one another.

To reiterate, the value of this discourse is twofold. It is *deconstructive* in that it helps Black people to understand the many forces, especially White culture, that have shaped Black sexuality. It is also *constructive* in that it seeks to provide more life-enhancing views and attitudes concerning Black sexuality. Forming a sexual discourse of resistance is a necessary first step toward Black people gaining agency over their own sexuality; without such a discourse, the discourse of White culture is free to penetrate Black life.

To further clarify the urgent mandate for a sexual discourse of resistance, we will explore more specifically the ways in which White culture has perhaps left its mark upon certain aspects of Black sexuality, specifically Black self-esteem, Black relationships, and Black spirituality.

The Impact upon Black Self-Esteem

The "pain of generations" of White cultural exploitation has been etched onto who Black people are, men and especially women, particularly as they regard their embodied Black selves. Cheryl Townsend Gilkes makes the point when she says, "African Americans' existential ambivalence about their bodies may be the most personally painful legacy of slavery and racial oppression in the United States."[28] She goes on to point out that this ambivalence is perhaps most intense for the Black woman. Toinette Eugene makes a similar point:

> Worse yet, though, the greatest dehumanization or violence that actually can occur in racist and/or sexist situations happens when persons of the rejected racial- or gender-specific group begin to internalize the judgments made by others and become convinced of their own personal inferiority. Obviously, the most affected and thus dehumanized victims of this experience are black women.[29]

As shown in the previous chapter, being of the "wrong" color *and* gender caused Black women to be uniquely humiliated and violated. They were considered other than "females" and hence available for White male rape and debauchery. As also shown in the previous chapter, such humiliation continues for Black women, as they are still viewed as outside the norm of American female beauty and are treated as Jezebels. Black women are entrapped by a history that has devalued who they are as *Black* women. They continue to wear the scars of a White cultural humiliation that debases their womanhood. They harbor the pain of someone else's devaluation of their color, hair, hips, noses, and basically the way they move, live, and have their being. They bear within their psyches the open wounds of the violence perpetrated against their bodies.

There are numerous testimonies from Black women of their struggles to accept their Black womanhood in a world that devalues them. There is no more poignant testimony, however, than that of a South African woman. Though not African American, her story epitomizes the devastating impact of White culture on Black bodies, especially in the absence of a mitigating discourse. She tells her story this way:

> I carry in my body the scars of violence, of generations of slavery, rape and murder. I carry in my body the scars of violence. How

does this affect the way I walk, the way I look, the way I relate to others? I will take just one example: I have spent some months being intensely self-conscious about my body (a bit belatedly since I have been dancing for seventeen years), but anyway through working with it I discovered that I sit with my shoulders hunched. Raised and angry voices make me hunch further. So it took me all my life to realize that even though a hand was never raised to me at home I walk and sit like a child who grows up in a violent household, like someone who tries not to be noticed in case they get hit. My stance is inherited, for how many generations I cannot say. But I began to understand the difference between walking like a slave and walking like a free woman. And those hunched shoulders affected my stance; suddenly I realized how much time I spent looking down, and how little I spent looking upwards to the Light. As I practiced walking tall, I discovered how much pain I had been walking around with in my backbone, the pain of generations.[30]

Without a sexual discourse of resistance the legacy of one woman's pain cannot be confronted. The absence of such a discourse means far too many Black men and women are left to feel ashamed of their bodies. They have limited avenues for discovering that the pain, ambivalence, and/or shame they feel are shared experiences generated by a history of exploitation. They are left to negotiate by themselves the burden of years of humiliation heaped upon them by a White culture that suggests that Black physiognomy is a sign of inferiority and wantonness. They are left with little help in their quest to love themselves. The impact of such unactualized self-love has been devastating for the Black community.

From 1985 to 1986, *Washington Post* journalist Leon Dash conducted a study on Black teenage pregnancy in Anacostia, a section of Washington, D.C., formally known as Washington Highlands. After living in this community for several months and conducting repeated interviews with a group of teenage girls, Dash released what were then startling findings in a six-day series in the *Post*. His findings revealed that nearly one-fourth of the twelve-, thirteen-, and fourteen-year-old girls studied wanted to become pregnant. As one teenager put it, "None of this childbearing is an accident!"[31] Recalling his teenage years, a young Black male even admitted that it was important for the adolescent boys to get girls pregnant so that they could "feel like a man."[32] Teenage pregnancy continues to be an ever-present concern for the Black community. Though the gap between White and Black teenagers is reported closing, far too many Black teenagers are participating in unsafe sexual activity and, hence, bearing children.

The Black community is also plagued by the occurrence of what some have termed homicidal suicides, that is Black teenagers, especially males, killing other Black teenagers, especially males. For instance, by 1991 homicide was the leading cause of death for Black males between the ages of fifteen and thirty-four. Unfortunately, most of the deaths occur at the hands of another Black male. The situation among Black males is so disturbing that some have gone so far as to label Black males an "endangered species." It is evident that there is a disturbing genocidal pattern of behavior in the Black community, especially among Black teens. Yet the solution to this problem is not as evident.

Why is it that teenagers continue to engage in the kind of sexual activity that leads not only to pregnancy, but also to life-threatening diseases such as AIDS? Why is it so easy for Black teenagers, particularly males, to maim and kill those who look like them? Why do young Black women and men seem to have so little regard for their Black selves that they easily fall prey to crime and drug abuse? Without a doubt, far too many Black youth live in conditions that are life-negating. They are trapped in poverty's cycle of indecent housing, substandard schools, lack of health care, inadequate employment opportunities, and nonexistent recreational options. This means that the struggle to eradicate the systems and structures that breed these socioeconomic genocidal conditions must be unrelenting. It also means that Black teenagers must be properly equipped with the tools to strive for life under circumstances that would deny that life.

Essential to their striving is an unadulterated self-love. They must be able to love themselves in the midst of a society that disdains their blackness. In a society where Black people are bombarded by White cultural messages that decry Black sexuality and disparage blackness, it is not enough for Black church and community leaders to instruct our children to simply say no to sex, drugs, or other destructive behavior. The Black church and community must engage in a sexual discourse of resistance that empowers Black women and men to celebrate and to love their Black embodied selves. Such a discourse would help Black people to distinguish who they are from what White culture suggests of them. It would help them name the pain of White culture's racialized sexual humiliation so that they could move on to a place of healing and regard for their body-selves. West explains it this way:

[The] demythologizing of black sexuality is crucial for black
America because much of black self-hatred and self-contempt has
to do with the refusal of many black Americans to love their own
black bodies — especially their black noses, hips, lips, and hair.
Just as many white Americans view black sexuality with disgust,
so do many black Americans.[33]

A powerful passage from Toni Morrison's novel Beloved, placed on the
lips of her character Baby Suggs Holy during the tyranny of slavery,
captures what must be an essential message of a Black sexual discourse
of resistance:

"Here," she said, "in this here place, we flesh; flesh that weeps,
laughs; flesh that dances on bare feet in grass. Love it. Love it
hard. Yonder they do not love your flesh. They despise it. They
don't love your eyes; they'd just as soon pick em out. No more do
they love the skin on your back. Yonder they flay it. And O my
people they do not love your hands. Those they only use, tie,
bind, chop off and leave empty. Love your hands! Love them.
Raise them up and kiss them. Touch others with them, pat them
together, stroke them on your face 'cause they don't love that
either. You got to love it, You! . . . This is flesh I'm talking about
here. Flesh that need to be loved. Feet that need to rest and to
dance; backs that need support; shoulders that need arms, strong
arms I'm telling you. And O my people, out yonder, hear me, they
do not love your neck unnoosed and straight. So love your neck;
put a hand on it, grace it, stroke it and hold it up. And all your
inside parts that they'd just as soon slop for hogs, you got to love
them. The dark, dark liver — love it, love it, and the beat and
beating heart, love that too. More than eyes or feet. More than
lungs that have yet to draw free air. More than your life-holding
womb and your life-giving private parts, hear me now, love your
heart.[34]

If the Black community could communicate such a message, Black
women and men, especially the young, could unabashedly celebrate
their sensual and corporeal selves and Black teenagers would no doubt
be less likely to engage in self-destructive, self-hating behaviors. Without resistance, the discourse of White culture will continue to succeed
in wreaking havoc on the bodies and minds of Black people. Black
self-esteem will continue to fall prey too easily to White culture's historical and consistent sexual degradation of Black men and women.

Unfortunately, self-esteem has not been the only causality; male/female relationships have also been damaged.

Black Male/Female Relationships

That there is tension in Black male/female, romantic and nonromantic, relationships is clear. Evidence of these strained relationships is seen in various aspects of Black life, from Black literature and art to the Black church. A review of some recent popular movies made by Black men and women, along with reactions to these films, suggests generally troubled relationships between males and females in the Black community.

Many Black male filmmakers appear to be content to follow the legacy of Melvin Van Peebles and others, whose 1960s films and plays, such as *Sweetback's Bad Black Ass,* presented Black women as sexual objects to be abused and exploited. To be sure, in Black male films Black women have not been presented with any degree of consistency as multidimensional persons defined by other than their genitals. Spike Lee's career-launching film, *She's Gotta Have It,* exemplifies the genre of Black male films that diminishes the humanity of Black women. Though in this film Lee may have intended to present a critical look at Black female and especially Black male sexuality, the film actually perpetuates White cultural norms and stereotypes. Without much development of the main character, Nola Darling, the film preserves the notion that Black women are overly sexualized beings who find fulfillment through sexual activity, even when that includes rape. In her penetrating review of the film, bell hooks explains:

> Nola has no personality. She is shallow, vacuous, empty. Her one claim to fame is that she likes to fuck. In the male pornographic imagination she could be described as "pure pussy," that is to say that her ability to perform sexually is the central, defining aspect of her identity....
>
> Filmmaker Spike Lee challenges and critiques notions of black male sexuality while presenting a very typical perspective on black female sexuality.[35]

She's Gotta Have It was not the last of Lee's films to portray Black females in racially sexist ways. While admittedly exploring very significant themes in Black life and culture, films such as *School Daze, Jungle Fever,* and *Mo' Better Blues* are greatly marred by their portrayal of many of their Black female characters as sexualized beings waiting to be exploited by Black men. hooks says of *School Daze:*

> A scene in Spike Lee's film *School Daze* depicts an all black party where everyone is attired in swimsuits dancing — doing the butt. It is one of the most compelling moments in the film. The black "butts" on display are unruly and outrageous. They are not the still bodies of the female slave made to appear as mannequin. They are not a silenced body. Displayed as playful cultural nationalist resistance, they challenge assumptions that the black body, its skin color and shape, is a mark of shame. Undoubtedly the most transgressive and provocative moment in *School Daze,* ... [i]ts potential to disrupt and challenge notions of black bodies, specifically female bodies, was undercut by the overall sexual humiliation and abuse of black females in the film.[36]

Mo' Better Blues rounds out its presentation of Black women by also depicting them as emasculating mothers. hooks comments:

> Spike Lee's recent film *Mo' Better Blues* is another tragic vision of contemporary black heterosexuality. ... It focuses on a world of black male homosocial bonding where black women are seen primarily as sex objects. Even when they have talent, ... they must still exchange their sexual favors for recognition. ...
>
> [Bleek's (the main character)] life crisis is resolved by the reinscription of a patriarchal paradigm. ... The film suggests Bleek has no choice and can only reproduce the same family narrative from which he emerged, effectively affirming the appropriateness of a nuclear family paradigm where women as mothers restrict black masculinity, black male creativity, and fathers hint at the possibility of freedom.[37]

Lee has not been the only culprit among Black male filmmakers in making use of stereotypic and demeaning portraits of Black women that resonate with White cultural portrayals of them. In spite of its penetrating look into the lives of urban Black males, John Singleton's *Boyz in the Hood* (which some considered a brilliant film) continued the degradation of Black women. In this film Black mothers were viewed at once as emasculating, overbearing, and/or irresponsible, while other Black women were sexually exploited and causally referred to as "bitches" and "hoes." Singleton followed this film with *Poetic Justice,* which again portrayed Black women in a disquieting fashion. Michael Dyson calls these depictions "shameful and stereotypical."[38]

If films made by Black men manifest trouble between Black men and women, so too do those based on texts written by Black women. The 1995 film *Waiting to Exhale,* based on Terry Macmillan's novel, exemplifies this. In this movie, against the backdrop of troubled relationships with men, four Black women discover their individual strength as well as the power of Black sistering. This film depicts from a Black female perspective the loves and troubles of Black male/female relationships. The release of *Waiting to Exhale* caused an almost immediate outcry from many Black men who felt that the movie unfairly bashed them. Though not in agreement with this sentiment, Dyson explains that "[m]any complained that black men were taking a drubbing. That sisters needed to give brothers a break."[39] Such outcry was similar to that surrounding Ntozoke Shange's chorepoem and play *For Colored Girls* and the release on the big screen of Alice Walker's *The Color Purple.*

Black male responses to these movies are foreboding, as they suggest that many Black men are unwilling to hear the stories of Black women. They attest to the almost dogged refusal of some Black men to recognize and appreciate the complexity of Black women's experiences in attempting to voice and celebrate their Black womanhood and sisterhood.

The critical response to various Black female movies also signals the insidious sexism present within the Black community. For while Black men deplored their own depiction in films, they have remained virtually silent, with some noted exceptions, concerning the "shameless and stereotypic" manner in which Black women have been portrayed in Black male films. Their silence suggests that their own attitudes concerning Black women are not much different than those displayed by the Black male film characters, who sexually, physically, verbally, and emotionally abuse Black women. Overall, from films made by Black men to those based on works written by Black women, the Black film industry has provided a good barometer of the tensions and antagonisms that shadow female/male relationships in the Black community.

This strain between female and male is also seen in the social and political realities of Black life. Events like the Clarence Thomas/Anita Hill hearings exposed the "trust" gap between Black men and women. Many Black men, for instance, refused to give Hill's charges of sexual harassment any merit. Instead, they saw her as a "treacherous, jealous" Black woman trying to bring down a Black man. Black women, in contrast, were more apt to see the merit of Hill's charges and were readier to acknowledge that Black women are oftentimes victims of sexual harassment, even at the hands of Black men.

Another public incident involving a Black woman and man caused similar reactions. After Marion Barry, the District of Columbia's Black mayor, was arrested on drug-related charges while in the room of a Black woman who had been employed by the FBI, many Black men donned T-shirts saying "It was the bitch's fault." A similar attitude was displayed by the National Baptist Convention's reaction to Desiree Washington's rape charges against Mike Tyson. The official leadership of the Black denomination supported Tyson while remaining silent about Washington's victimization and vilification. Each of these events — the Thomas hearing, the Barry arrest, and the Tyson case — shows how easy it is for Black men to accept the image of Black women as traitors and Jezebels. At the same time, they signify the deep rift of mistrust and misunderstanding that separates the two groups.

No social/political event in Black life reveals this rift more than the Million Man March in 1995. For all the good that this march may have done to bring Black men together to affirm themselves as responsible beings, it also exposed the schism between Black men and women. While many Black women supported the rightness of Black men coming together to affirm themselves and to take responsibility for their actions and their communities, other Black women loudly denounced the march. They resented the exclusion of Black women who, they felt, were given only ceremonial, tokenizing roles. They felt that once again Black women were being slapped in the face and unappreciated by the very men they had so long stood by and fought for. Black women also argued that the march only sharpened the schisms between Black men and women, especially as it did not offer a serious womanist or feminist analysis of the social and moral problems that plague the Black community. As a result, they saw the march as only a platform of rhetoric in support of Black men's right to patriarchal privileges heretofore granted only to White men.

Clearly, there is trouble between Black men and women. While individuals may enjoy healthy, mutual relationships of respect, the Black community remains plagued by antagonism between the sexes. Although open dialogue concerning gender relations is a necessary first step in ameliorating this tension, this dialogue has been slow in coming. The question is, Why?

To confront the issue of strained male/female relationships in the Black community would mean acknowledging the presence of sexism within that community. Black men and some Black women refuse to confront this issue and thus relinquish privileges that accrue from gender-biased systems and structures. But even more daunting for many in the Black community is the fact that a serious confrontation with sexism implies the even more difficult discussion of Black sexuality. The multifarious nature of sexism is inextricably connected to matters of sexuality. Open discussion, using a sexual discourse of resistance, is a crucial first step in frustrating the culture and structures of gender inequity within the Black community and in mending Black male/female relationships. Such a discourse would provide Black men and women with the opportunity to reflect upon the ways in which they have — wittingly or unwittingly — internalized the images of Black women as Jezebels or emasculating mothers and have accepted White female standards of beauty. Cornel West speaks to this when he says:

> I do believe that deep down in the depths of the Black male psyche is a struggle with taking seriously the beauty of Black women. The ideals of White beauty, when it comes to women, are so deeply inscribed in every male psyche, Black and White, that many brothers do have problems acknowledging Black beauty, and by beauty I don't simply mean physical beauty.[40]

Sexual discourse would also enable Black men and women to confront their complicity in fostering notions of Black hypersexuality, especially when it comes to Black men. hooks says, "Many black people have passively absorbed narrow representations of black masculinity, perpetuated stereotypes, myths, and offered one-dimensional accounts. Contemporary black men have been shaped by these representations."[41] A comprehensive discussion of Black sexuality would prompt Black people to face head on the degree to which their perceptions of femininity and masculinity have been shaped by the ideology of a White patriarchal culture. Black men's and women's depictions of each other in films and music, as well as their responses to public events, certainly suggest the imprint of White cultural stereotypes. By carefully examining the relationships among sex, race, and power in America and the way they have been influenced by the sexual politics of White culture, Black people can begin to unravel the messiness of their own intimate relationships. Patricia Hill Collins speaks to this:

Much of the antagonism African-American women and men feel may stem from an unstated resentment toward Eurocentric gender ideology and against one another as enforcers of the dichotomous sex role inherent in the ideology. Eurocentric gender ideology objectifies both sexes so that when Black men see Black women as nothing more than mammies, matriarchs, or Jezebels, or even if they insist on placing African-American women on the same queenly pedestal reserved for white women, they objectify not only Black women but their own sexuality.[42]

An understanding of the sexual politics of White culture will also allow Black people to begin to divest themselves of notions of Black freedom that equate male privilege with "authentic" blackness. A comprehensive sexual discourse of resistance would undoubtedly probe why the Black community has so often likened gaining a certain standard of "manhood" with Black freedom. During the Black power movement of the 1960s, for instance, the Black man's ability to practice his manhood according to White patriarchal norms became a goal of Black liberation struggles, even though such manhood meant the subjugation of Black women. Again, hooks comments:

> Contemporary black power movement[s] made synonymous black liberation and the effort to create a social structure wherein black men could assert themselves as patriarchs, controlling community, family and kin. On one hand, black men expressed contempt for white men yet they also envied them their access to patriarchal power.[43]

Even Black male ministers and theologians equated Black liberation with gaining Black manhood. A June 13, 1969, statement released by the National Committee of Black Churchmen said:

> We now commit ourselves to the risks of affirming the dignity of black personhood. We do this as men and as black Christians. This is the message of Black theology. In the words of Eldridge Cleaver:
>
> > We shall have our manhood.
> > We shall have it or the earth will be leveled by our efforts to gain it.[44]

Why have Black manhood and Black freedom so often been linked in the Black community? Again, this question cannot be adequately addressed until Black people comprehend how White culture has manipulated Black male and female sexuality to such a degree that the acquisition of "manhood according to patriarchal standards" has become a precious commodity for many in the Black community.

An open, frank sexual discourse of resistance is crucial to Black people's ability to penetrate the impact of White culture's exploitative sexual politics upon their personal and interpersonal matters. Moreover, until the sexual politics of White culture is exposed as buttressing White patriarchal hegemony, Black men and women will not be able to dismantle the interlocking structures of race, gender, class, and sexual oppression that place so much stress on Black relationships. Again, this makes the need for a sexual discourse of resistance urgent. If Black men and women are truly committed to one another and hence to freedom for the entire Black community, they can no longer avoid penetrating the sexual politics of Black life, especially as they have been infringed upon by the sexual politics of White culture.

The repercussions of White culture on sexual discourse in the Black community are seen not only on Black self-esteem and male/female relationships, but also on Black spirituality. Though the relationship between sexuality and spirituality will be looked at in much more detail in chapter 5, we will take a brief look at this topic here in order to understand the pervasive impact of White culture on Black sexuality.

BLACK SPIRITUALITY

White culture's sexual exploitation has had a profound effect on Black spirituality and the Black church. The manner in which Black women are treated in many Black churches reflects the Western Christian tradition's notion of women as evil and its notions of Black women as Jezebels and seducers of men. For instance, there are still Black churches that require women to cover their legs with a blanket when sitting in a pew so they will not distract men. This excuse that Black women are too sexually distracting is also commonly used to keep these women out of the pulpit and ordained ministry. But the mythology of Black women as Jezebels is perhaps most implied in the treatment of unwed mothers. In many Black churches unwed mothers are publicly chastised and made to repent in front of the whole congregation while the fathers are often ignored. This humiliating sexist ritual harks back to early Black church expectations that Black women should remain chaste after joining the church, a church that all the while said nothing about the sexual conduct of Black men. This double standard is hauntingly reminiscent of the logic used by White men who fathered children by Black women during the antebellum and postbellum period. These men were not held accountable for these children, who were seen as the sole responsibility of the mother because, according to White logic, it was the seductive, passionate manner of the Black woman that caused the sexual encounter.

As these White cultural stereotypes have invaded the sacred and spiritual space of Black people, they have had an even more pernicious impact upon Black spirituality. Spirituality involves more than worship or prayer life or simply going to church. Spirituality concerns a person's connection to God and, thus, inevitably involves her or his sexuality. As indicated earlier in this book, sexuality is that fundamental dimension of human beings that governs intimate, sensual, affective, emotional, and sexual relationships. Human sexuality and spirituality are inextricably linked because both involve a person's relationship to God. Toinette Eugene recognizes the bond between sexuality and spirituality when she says: "Spirituality is no longer identified simply with asceticism, mysticism, the practice of virtue, and methods of prayer. Spirituality, i.e. the human capacity to be self-transcending, relational, and freely committed, encompasses all of life, including our human sexuality."[45]

Many African cultures long embraced the intrinsic connection between spirituality and sexuality. This was evidenced by their resistance to dualistic distinctions between the sacred and the secular, the soul and the body. There is no radical break in most African traditions between the spiritual and fleshly realms: all that is of the earthly realm is God's and is sacred. As Peter Paris observes in his study of African spirituality, "secularity has no reality in the African experience."[46] The human body and the entirety of the human being are viewed as part of the sacred, as part of the divine, including the human being as a sexual and relational being. This is why many African cultures did not view sexual intercourse as bad or evil, but celebrated this sacred part of life.

In the final analysis, human sexuality makes human relationships possible — including the relationship to the divine. The quality of a person's relationship to God, therefore, hinges in many ways on her or his awareness and appreciation of her or his own sexuality. To be estranged from one's sexuality in all of its dimensions portends a diminished relationship with God. In this way White culture has left its inimical mark upon Black spirituality.

Unable to celebrate and appreciate their embodied Black selves, Black men and women have often been unable to fully know the image of God that is theirs to bear and show forth to the world. How, for instance, are we to resolve the contradiction between being created in the image of God and being made to feel that everything about who we are as Black people is inferior? Such a contradiction typically renders a person incapable of seeing her/himself as a reflection of the divine. Instead one sees oneself as less than God or as White culture has intended for Black people to see themselves — as an affront to the image of God. (More will be said about this later.)

White culture not only has impeded Black people's ability to embrace themselves, but also has interfered with their ability to know God. In order to resist the discourse of White culture that suggests that Black is bad and contrary to God, Black people must engage in a sexual discourse that maintains the opposite. Such a strategy has the power to foil the goals of White culture. A discourse that resists White culture can encourage and empower Black people to appreciate their own Black bodies and to celebrate every aspect of their blackness as a gift and sign of God. Such a discourse can pave the way for Black women and men to recognize the image of God that is in them and finally to say, "I found God in myself and I loved her [him] fiercely." If the Black community does not engage in such a discourse, the discourse of White culture will remain free to corrupt Black men's and women's recognition of their own divine beauty and significance. Without such a discourse Black people will be handicapped in seeing the face of God that is indeed their face.

CONCLUSIONS

This chapter has shown how White culture's sexual characterization and exploitation of Black people has had a far-reaching and deleterious impact on Black lives. This attack has provided a gateway for the contamination of all of Black sexuality, from Black people's relationships with themselves to their relationship with God. But perhaps the most insidious result of the White cultural attack upon Black sexuality is that it has rendered the Black community practically silent in terms of sexual discourse. Such a silence further assures the success of White culture in nurturing White patriarchal hegemony. As long as the Black community refuses to engage in a frank, consistent sexual discourse of resistance, Black sexuality in all of its complexity will continue to be ravaged by the sexual politics of White culture, and the Black community will be handicapped in addressing significant matters of life and death for Black people.

This leads us to the topic that initiated my study of Black sexuality — homophobia.

CHAPTER 4

Homophobia and Heterosexism in the Black Church and Community

— I can love the sinner, but not the sin.

— Homosexuality is an abomination.

— To be gay goes against nature.

— If we were supposed to be homosexual, God would have created Adam and Steve, not Adam and Eve.

— I don't mind gay people, but why do they have to be so vocal and pushy about their rights?

— Homosexuality is a White thing.

— Africa did not have homosexuals before Europeans went there.

— Homosexuality is detrimental to the Black family.

I often hear students pronounce these assertions and similar ones in my classes anytime we address the issue of homophobia in the Black church and community. In my ten years of teaching at the Howard University School of Divinity, no topic has seemed to touch more of a raw nerve than homosexuality. During classroom discussions, many students seem to have no inhibitions in expressing their disgust with gay and lesbian sexuality. They speak about gay and lesbian persons as sinners, abominations, perverts, and diseased. They often carry on their tirades as if gay and lesbian people do not deserve love and respect as human beings, although they paradoxically proclaim that as Christians they love everybody. Many of the students express themselves with little regard for whether or not they are inflicting deep pain on other students, gay or nongay, in the class. Because the discussion surrounding homophobia is frequently so venomous, I find myself questioning the wisdom of including it in my syllabus. But year after year I do, convinced that homophobia is a subject that the Black community must confront. And, as will become clearer, I am also increasingly convinced that this is an issue that no Christian theologian, especially a womanist theologian, can avoid with integrity.

Yet virtual silence — beyond moral invectives and self-righteous assertions — has characterized the Black community's consideration of gay and lesbian sexuality. Why is the Black community so averse to reflecting seriously on issues surrounding gay and lesbian sexuality? Why is the subject so particularly burdensome? Why does the mention of homosexuality often create acrimonious debate? How is it that a church community so committed to racial justice can be so intransigent about gay and lesbian rights? The answers to these questions seem submerged in the reasoning behind Black homophobic attitudes and practices, which, in turn, stem from the complexity of Black people's oppression at the hands of White culture.

Given the intensity of feelings toward homosexuality in the Black community, many have suggested that homophobia is more virulent and rampant among Black people than in the wider heterosexist American society. Though the rhetoric surrounding Black homophobia may suggest that this is the case, the facts do not bear this out. On the one hand, there have been no persons more ardently homophobic than White televangelists Pat Robertson and Jerry Falwell or political commentator Pat Buchanan. More recently, Senate Majority Leader Trent Lott's remarks comparing homosexuals to alcoholics, kleptomaniacs, and sex addicts has ignited a vigorous campaign by the religious right urging homosexuals to "be cured."

On the other hand, while homophobia is certainly pervasive in the Black community, there have been significant Black voices that have forthrightly supported gay and lesbian rights. Civil rights leaders such as Jesse Jackson, Joseph Lowery, Coretta Scott King, and Benjamin Chavis have all publicly decried discriminatory policies or behaviors toward gay and lesbian persons. At the same time they have supported agendas promoting gay and lesbian rights. In addition, the Congressional Black Caucus as a body, as well as its individual members, has consistently rejected legislation that would discriminate against gay and lesbian persons, and it has openly supported gay and lesbian rights.

If the Black community is not more homophobic than the wider heterosexist society of which it is a part, then why do both Whites and Blacks often assert that the Black community is hyperhomophobic? Why does it often appear from casual observation that the Black community is much more rigid and zealous than other communities about its antigay and antilesbian sentiments? Again, the answer to these questions is found in the history of Black people's oppression. While the Black church and community share the logic of others who denounce homosexuality, their particular history of White racist oppression and sexual exploitation makes Black homophobia appear even more passionate, trenchant, and unyielding. Angela Davis acknowledges the role of White culture in shaping the Black church's response to homosexuality:

> The fear of homosexuality perpetuated by the church is related to a generalized fear of sexuality. This fear of sexuality takes on new meaning when considered in light of the fact that the freedom to choose sexual partners was one of the most powerful distinctions between the condition of slavery and the postemancipation status of African Americans.[1]

Essentially, Black people's views toward homosexuality must be understood in light of their responses to sexuality in general, particularly as those responses have been refracted by White culture. Given that, it is important to understand that the complexity of Black homophobia cannot be adequately covered in a single chapter. It is a topic that warrants extensive study, as homophobia is manifested in various ways throughout the Black community, from the church to popular hip-hop and gangsta culture. Most recently, for instance, Angie and Debbie Winans created controversy throughout the Black community when they released a song that denounced homosexuality, "It's Not Natural." A comprehensive analysis of the nature of Black homophobia, as well as the reality that gives birth to a song like "It's Not Natural," deserves its own book. This chapter, therefore, does not propose to provide a complete analysis of Black homophobia; instead, it will outline the general contours of this analysis as it seeks to understand the relationship between Black homophobia and Black oppression, particularly the exploitation of Black sexuality. This chapter will also explore the role of a sexual discourse of resistance in addressing Black homophobia.

THE BIBLE AND HOMOSEXUALITY

Not unlike others who condemn homosexuality, the Black community appeals to the Bible. On numerous occasions when discussing the

issue of homophobia, my Black interlocutors have ended their arguments with some version of "The bottom line is that the Bible says
homosexuality is wrong." Whether they are churchgoers or not, Black
people often argue that the Bible makes clear that homosexuality is a
sin. By invoking biblical authority they place a sacred canopy, a divine
sanction, over their views toward gay and lesbian persons. This canopy
renders homophobia practically intractable. The Bible becomes, then, a
tool for censoring a group of people, in this case, gay men and lesbians.

The irony is, however, that the Bible does not present as clear a position on homosexuality as is often self-righteously asserted. The meaning
of the biblical stories customarily referred to as proof against homosexual practices has generally been misconstrued or distorted. Biblical
scholars have painstakingly shown that the Leviticus Holiness Codes
(Lev. 18:22; 20:13), the story of Sodom and Gomorrah (Gen. 19:1–9),
and Paul's Epistle to the Romans (1:26–27) do not present a compelling case against homoeroticism.[2] These scholars have also pointed
out that neither the words nor the actions of Jesus, as recorded in
the Gospels, suggest an antigay or antilesbian stance. In fact, the New
Testament shows Jesus to be virtually indifferent about matters of sexuality. When Jesus discussed sexual issues, he was typically making a
wider point. For example, Jesus used the example of committing adul-
tery "in one's heart" to point to the role of intention in committing
sin. When confronted with actual adulterers, Jesus recommended no
apparent punishment but, instead, suggested that self-examination was
of equal concern (John 8:3–11). The only sexual issue that seemed of
grave importance to Jesus was fidelity, in that he prohibited divorce
except in cases of infidelity. Jesus made no pronouncement and certainly no condemnation concerning homosexuality. As John Boswell
accurately points out: "No effort is made to elaborate a comprehensive sexual ethic: Jesus and his followers simply responded to situations
and questions requiring immediate attention."[3] Therefore, as is the case
with the Old Testament, the New Testament provides no indisputable
position on homosexuality.

Given the Bible's unclear view, to use the Bible to support a position on homosexuality would seem untenable. Yet scripture is often the
cornerstone of homophobia in the Black community. Why is this the
case? It is probably safe to say that homophobic prejudice has driven
our reading of the Bible, as opposed to the Bible shaping homophobia.
Biased eyes often turn to the biblical witness in support of the bias, particularly when communities attempt to justify their oppression of other

human beings. The Bible then becomes a tool of oppression and is taken up as a weapon to censor the behavior and restrict the life possibilities of others. This has been true for White exploitation of Black people. The White slaveholding class interpreted the Bible in such a way to suggest that God ordained slavery and that blackness was a curse. Fortunately, Black people were able to hear the Bible for themselves and to realize that such an interpretation was more reflective of the White slaveholders' desire for privilege than of what was found in the Bible.

With such a history of the Bible being used against them, it seems abhorrent for Black people to be so steadfast in their use of the Bible against other Black persons, in this case, gay men and lesbians. How can a community that has suffered under an oppression covered with a sacred canopy inflict the same oppression upon others? How can such a community be so unwilling to reevaluate its use of biblical authority? How can it remain so closed to new understandings of problematic texts?

While there is certainly no excuse for placing a sacred canopy over any type of injustice or human misery, Black people's utilization of the Bible to damn homosexuality is somewhat understandable in light of their history of oppression. It is not simply a matter of a bigoted refusal to be "enlightened" by biblical scholarship or of a narrow-minded literalism. Black biblical scholars are beginning to discern that Black people's approaches to biblical texts bespeak a judicious sense of biblical authority born during the period of enslavement and honed throughout their history of struggle in America. Two well-known Black biblical scholars, Vincent Wimbush and Renita Weems, provide extended explications of how the Bible functions in the Black community. Their understanding of biblical authority as conceived in the Black community has important implications for Black people's use of the Bible in supporting homophobia.

The Black Biblical Tradition

Wimbush postulates that "a history of African Americans' historical readings of the Bible is likely to reflect their historical self-understandings — as Africans in America."[4] He explains that the Bible provided African Americans with a "language world" that helped them to negotiate their "strange existence." "In short," he argues, "the Bible became a 'world' into which African Americans could retreat, a 'world' they could identify with, draw strength from, and in fact manipulate for self-affirmation."[5]

Renita Weems looks specifically at the way in which African American women have appropriated biblical texts in light of their use to support both racial and gender inequity. She challenges biblical scholars to realize that the influence of the Bible in African American lives, especially in the lives of African American women, "involves more than the reader's lack of sophistication, or a slavish dogmatic devotion to the Bible."[6]

Both Wimbush and Weems recognize that the use of the Bible to justify Africans' enslavement has clearly impacted Black people's approach to biblical texts. Wimbush says that the enslaved men and women initially reacted to such usage with an "admixture of rejection, suspicion, and awe."[7] They rejected any notion of "book religion" because of the way their enslavers utilized this particular book and, most notably, because of their "well-established and elaborate" oral traditions. Yet "the fact that those who were conquering the New World were 'Bible Christians' was not at all lost on the Africans,"[8] says Wimbush. They were very cognizant of the power found in the Bible. Despite the fact that they were not permitted to learn to read or write or to encounter the Bible independently from their enslavers, the enslaved Africans found a way to know this "powerful" book for themselves. Rendered basically illiterate in terms of English by their slavery, they did this primarily through an oral/aural tradition of sermons, songs, and public readings. Weems points out, "What the slavemasters did not foresee, however, was that the very material they forbade the slaves from touching and studying with their hands and eyes, the slaves learned to claim and study through the powers of listening and memory."[9] A distinct understanding of biblical authority emerged as part of this oral/aural tradition of transmission, and it determined two things: the stories that would be transmitted and how they would be interpreted.

The oral/aural tradition is selective about which biblical texts are passed on. Stories from scripture that seemed to support enslavement and that were most used by the enslavers held little significance for the enslaved men and women and did not survive in the oral/aural tradition. The stories that did survive were those that were compatible with Black life and freedom, and, in time, they comprised the oral/aural Black biblical tradition. Weems clarifies, "Where the Bible has been able to capture the imagination of African American women [and men], it has been and continues to be able to do so because significant portions speak to the deepest aspirations of oppressed people for freedom, dignity, justice, and vindication."[10]

Essentially the oral/aural tradition attests to the creation of a "canon within the canon" for the Black community. Certain texts and stories became favorites and thus have been most often recited in song, prayer, and testimony. Wimbush explains how "the occurrence of certain clusters of biblical materials over and over [is] significant especially in terms of the development of a 'canon.'"[11] He continues:

> [The enslaved Africans] were attracted primarily to the narratives of the Hebrew Bible dealing with the adventures of the Hebrews in bondage and escaping from bondage, to the oracles of the eighteenth-century prophets and their denunciation of social injustice and visions of social justice, and to the New Testament texts concerning the compassion, passion, and resurrection of Jesus. With these and other texts, the African American Christians laid the foundations for what can be seen as an emerging "canon."[12]

Indeed, the canon that initially emerged in the oral/aural tradition of the enslaved community appears to be germane today. Black spirituals, prayers, and testimony continue to reflect Black people's allegiance to particular texts that express the concern for the weak over the strong, or where the oppressed are set free and the despised are preferred. Most notably, the events and heroes of the Exodus story remain as central to contemporary Black faith as they were to enslaved religion. Repeatedly, and in various forms, Black church people refer to the victory of the Hebrew children over the mighty army of Pharaoh. They also give consistent jubilant and vivid testimony to David's humbling of the great Goliath, to Daniel being freed from the lions' den, to Jonah's release from the belly of the whale, and to the Hebrew children escaping from the fiery furnace.

Not only did the oral/aural tradition reflect a precise canon, but it also signaled a definite principle of interpretation. Weems says of this, "[T]he transmitters of the Bible in a slave culture rehearsed and interpreted the contents of the Bible as they saw fit."[13] To interpret as "they saw fit" typically meant that the enslaved men and women appropriated particular scriptural texts through the lens of their own experience. They interpreted the biblical stories in a manner that might shed light on their particular struggles for survival and freedom and that affirmed their faith in a God who was for them, not against them. As Wimbush puts it:

The interpretation was not controlled by the literal words of the texts, but by social experience. The texts were heard more than read; they were engaged as stories that seized and freed the imagination. Interpretation was therefore controlled by the freeing of the collective consciousness and imagination of the African slaves as they heard the biblical stories and retold them to reflect their actual social situation, as well as their visions for something different.[14]

To recapitulate, the way Black people have historically approached the Bible reveals an understanding of biblical authority that emerged out of and maintains an oral/aural tradition of biblical transmission. Those texts with authority in this tradition are ones that Black people consider compatible with their own struggle for life and freedom. This legacy of biblical authority has several implications that impact Black people's use of the Bible in relation to homosexuality.

Black Biblical Authority and Homosexuality

First, the prevalence of the oral/aural tradition suggests that the Bible to which Black people attest is the Bible that has been handed down to them in this tradition. Even though contemporary Black people may have more access to the written Bible than did their enslaved forebears, they do not necessarily embrace all texts as equally authoritative. This is evidenced by the stories Black people most commonly refer to in sermon, song, prayer, and testimony. The stories that had significance and authority in the past continue to have significance and authority today. As mentioned earlier, the Exodus event as well as the stories of David, Daniel, and others continue to be primary to Black faith. So while the oral/aural canon is not strictly closed, it is defined.

Black people's allegiance to this particular biblical tradition does not reflect a recalcitrant refusal to learn new things; rather, it is a testament to a faith and stories of faith that have served Black people well in their struggle for life and freedom. Any adjustments to this tradition need to emerge, therefore, from Black people's continuing experiences of struggle. These adjustments must resonate with Black people's faith in a God that nurtures Black well-being as it is defined by them.

Second, biblical stories continue to be understood in the way they have been handed down and interpreted. Thus, when questioned about a Bible story, it is not uncommon to hear a Black person reply, "Well, I only know what I was taught, and that is good enough for me." It is difficult to alter an interpretative biblical tradition that has served Black people so well.

Finally, the existence of the oral/aural tradition signifies that the Black community gives virtually no credence to White interpretations of the Bible, and for good reason. The way in which the enslavers used the Bible and the history of White biblical scholarship have caused many Black people to be suspicious of most biblical scholarship, of "book religion." In the minds of many Black people, biblical scholarship in general has been painted by the broad brush of European and Euro-American bias. Such bias is even reflected in the historical-critical approach to the Bible, which tends to "exalt a White cultural world view over other world views."[15] Black biblical scholar William Myers explains:

> The approach tends to lock the interpretative task in the past (e.g., in debates over authorial intent) while evading key contemporary issues like racism or intercultural dialogue. Although many of these works suggest that they cover the entire history of interpretation or that they address the full range of contemporary hermeneutical developments, in them one rarely finds any discussion of an African American interpretation of the Scriptures.[16]

Black people continue to rely more on their oral/aural tradition for appropriating the Bible than on what may come out of books about the Bible. Evidence of this is heard in numerous statements often made by Black men and women to the effect that "all that book learning [in relation to the Bible] has nothing to do with God."

What does this Black mistrust of White interpretation and the centrality of the oral/aural Black biblical tradition mean for the discussion of homosexuality in the Black community? It suggests that it is going to take more than "traditional" (White) biblical scholarship to persuade many in the Black community that homosexuality is not condemned by scripture. The mistrust of White people's handling of the Bible runs too deep for Black people, who, as a result, find it hard to accept White renderings of biblical texts on any matter, including sexuality. This means that the interpretation of certain texts (such as Lev. 18:22; 20:13; Gen. 19:1–9; and Rom. 1:26–27) will more likely reflect the homophobic understandings handed down in the Black oral/aural tradition than the exegetical findings of biblical scholars, especially since these traditional understandings seem to have served Black people well. (More will be said about this later.) So what does this suggest for the possibility of arresting Black people's use of the Bible as a sacred canopy for their homophobia? For it must not be thought that an understanding of the complexity of the Black biblical tradition that supports homophobia makes using the Bible to support human oppression any more tolerable.

In order to mitigate biblically based Black homophobia, a meaningful discussion of the Bible and sexuality, specifically homosexuality, will have to emerge from the Black community itself. It is a discussion that must take place within the wider context of Black people's own struggle for life and wholeness. It goes without saying that Black biblical scholars have particular responsibility in this area.

First, they are compelled to identify for Black people what has been a "biblical tradition of terror." This tradition is characterized by the use of various biblical texts to justify slavery, one of the most vile atrocities against humanity. In drawing attention to this "tradition of terror," these scholars must prompt Black people to make the connections between the way the Bible was used by Whites to terrorize them and the manner in which Black people use it to terrorize gay and lesbian persons. It must be made clear that participation in a biblical tradition of terror and allegiance to a biblical tradition that supports freedom are absolutely incompatible and hypocritical.

Next, Black biblical scholars must urge Black people to adopt a consistent "hermeneutic of suspicion" in relation to the way they use and interpret the biblical witness. This hermeneutic should be based on what has typically been the measure of biblical authority for Black people: Does the text support the life and freedom of all Black people? If Black men and women find themselves utilizing the Bible in a way that terrorizes other human beings, then they should disavow such usage. Most importantly, they should critically reevaluate the particular text that has led to such terror. It may be that certain offending texts will lose authority in the Black faith. Just as certain writings of Paul (especially those from Ephesians) have lost authority for many Black people, perhaps those that too easily lend themselves to the oppression of gay and lesbian persons should also be dismissed.

In light of the need for the Black faith community to reevaluate its understanding of certain texts, Black biblical scholars are obligated to find ways to communicate the complex and rich message of the scriptural witness on issues surrounding sexuality to Black people in a language and manner that maintains the integrity of the Black biblical oral/aural tradition. Black biblical scholars are challenged to advance the discussion of the Bible and homosexuality by employing the canon that has become authoritative for Black people. The Exodus event, for example, will have to be interpreted and understood in light of the experience of Black gay and lesbian persons.

Correspondingly, Black biblical scholars will have to confront the most significant component of Black biblical authority: biblical texts and interpretations of those texts that have gained authority in the Black community are those that resonate with the quest for Black survival and freedom. This principle of authority presents a special problem to the discussion of homosexuality, since homosexuality has long been viewed by many in the Black community as antithetical to Black well-being. Therefore any texts or interpretations of texts that would presume to support homoerotic behavior would more than likely remain nonauthoritative for the Black community and receive little hearing — unless homosexuality can be shown not to have a deleterious effect on Black life.

HOMOSEXUALITY AND THE WELL-BEING
OF THE BLACK COMMUNITY

Homosexuality: A White Thing

The fact that homosexuality can be considered harmful to Black well-being is inextricably related to the sexual exploitation and denigration of Black people by White culture. Because White culture racialized sex and "sexuated" race by equating blackness with sexual deviance, the Black community has been diligent in its efforts to sever the link between such deviance and blackness. Recognizing Black homophobia in part as a response to White sexual exploitation, Barbara Smith observes:

> One of the reasons that I have thought for homophobic attitudes among Black women is the whole sexual stereotyping used against Black people anyway, but especially women in relation to homosexuality — you know, the "Black bulldagger" image. Lesbianism is definitely about something sexual, a so-called deviant sexuality. So the way most Black women deal with it is to be just as rigid and closed about it as possible. White people don't have a sexual image that another oppressor community has put on them.[17]

Essentially, given a heterosexist society that considers homosexuality at best abnormal and at worse perverted, Black people have various ways to denounce homosexual practices in the Black community. There has been a vocal contingent, especially among nationalists and/or Afro-centrists, that has done this by asserting that homosexuality is a White thing. They argue that if Black people are indeed homosexual it is because they have come under the corrupting influence of White culture and values. In *The Isis Papers,* a popular book in the Black community, Frances Cress Welsing says: "Black male passivity, effeminization, bisexuality and homosexuality are being encountered increasingly by Black psychiatrists working with Black patient populations..., although [these conditions were] an almost nonexistent behavioral phenomenon amongst indigenous Blacks in Africa."[18]

Popular Afrocentrist Molefi Kete Asante shares Welsing's opinion, as he asserts that homosexuality is antagonistic to a commitment to the Black community since homosexuality reflects European decadence. He counsels male homosexuals: "We can no longer allow our social lives to be controlled by European decadence. The time has come for us to redeem our manhood through planned Afrocentric action. All brothers who are homosexuals should know that they too can become committed to the collective will."[19]

Yet these arguments that imply that homosexuality is anathema to African culture ignore numerous findings that suggest otherwise. In his movingly poignant account of being Black and gay in America, Keith Boykin provides an excellent summary of these findings:

> Modern anthropological evidence suggests the existence of homo-sexuality in virtually all human cultures, including those of Africa.... Scholars such as Warren Johansson, Geoff Puterbaugh, Stephen Murray, and Melville Herskovits have documented the reports of various sexual practices and family structures in black cultures. For example Portuguese sources indicate that homo-sexuality was common among the people of Angola at the time when colonists were scouting for slaves. Members of Nubian and Zulu cultures were known to assume alternative gender roles, women taking on important duties and men engaging in transvestite homosexuality. In 1937, Herskovits found that homo-sexuality was practiced by adolescents in Dahomey, and that some same-sex pairing persisted for life. S. F. Nadel reported having found "widespread homosexuality and transvestism" among the Otoro people in Sudan, as well as among the Moro, Nyima, and Tira. In his book *The Nuba* (1947), Nadel also documented mar-riages of Krongo *londo* and Masakin *tubele*. In a different example,

he revealed that attractive prepubescent boys served as pages to the chiefs of the Mossi people and assumed some female gender roles, including their style of dress. In Mombassa, Kenya, a dance known as *lelemama* served to identify and recruit married women into the lesbian subculture.[20]

In recognizing the close bonds that women have often formed, Audre Lorde cites the following story of a ninety-two-year-old Efik-Ibibio woman of Nigeria: "I had a woman friend to whom I revealed my secrets. She was very fond of keeping secrets to herself. We acted as husband and wife. We always moved hand in glove and my husband and hers knew about our relationship. The villagers nicknamed us twin sisters."[21]

The egregious claims that homosexuality is a White disease thus not only ignore the facts but also carelessly deny the humanity of many Black women and men. Barbara Smith puts it this way: "So often lesbianism and male homosexuality [are] talked about as a White disease within the Black community. It is just so negating of our lives."[22] Yet, regardless of the pain inflicted upon Black people, many persons alleging commitment to the life and freedom of the Black community continue to relinquish responsibility for their life-negating homophobic attitudes and practices with the easy excuse that homosexuality is a White thing.

Homosexuality: A Threat to the Black Family

Buttressing the belief that homosexuality is hostile to Black life is the argument that it erodes the Black family and concomitantly threatens Black masculinity. These arguments again appear viable in light of White cultural manipulation of Black sexuality. As noted above, one of the primary ways in which White culture has created an image of Black people as sexually deviant has been through its attacks on the Black family. Not only has the Black family been undermined by the structures of White racism in ways that have made it extremely difficult, if not at times impossible, for Black families (meaning, parents and children) to occupy the same households, but White culture has also attacked the models of family that Black people have erected to foster their survival. The Moynihan Report is a prime example of such an attack.

Recognizing the manipulation of the Black family by White culture, Rhonda Williams says:

Black families have long functioned as markers in the public imagination: they generally signify and manifest a morally problematic sexually [sic] agency, a cultural degeneracy. The conventional social scientific wisdom is clear: "the problem" is that so much black sexuality and kinship formation transgresses the boundaries of married (and therefore healthy) heterosexuality.[23]

One of the Black community's responses to this attack upon Black sexuality has been to advocate White family norms — that is, to espouse a family model more acceptable within a White patriarchal and heterosexist society. This model allows Black men to enjoy male privilege within the family structure. This becomes even more crucial in the Black community, perhaps, since the Black male is stripped of such privilege — by virtue of his blackness — in wider society. Though highly critical of this logic, activist and literary artist Cheryl Clarke recognizes the significance for the Black community of advocating White family norms:

The concept of the black family has been exploited since the publication of the infamous Moynihan report. . . . Because the insular, privatized nuclear family is upheld as the model of Western family stability, all other forms — for example, the extended family, the female-headed family, the lesbian family — are devalued. Many black people, especially middle-class black people, have accepted the male-dominated nuclear family model, though we have had to modify it because black women usually must work outside the home.[24]

Recognizing the relationship between "protecting" the Black family and homophobia, Rhonda Williams bluntly says:

Like Sapphire, black queers betray the quest for healthy black families, a regulated and normalized black sexuality. Whether viewed as the products of broken families or betrayers of family life together, black gays and lesbians are a potential anathema to straight African Americans whose resistance to racist narratives inspires them to "clean up" images of black sexuality.[25]

Nonheterosexual coupling has also been attacked for being nonproductive, and, as a result, homosexuality has been deemed genocidal for the Black race. Again, such an argument can appear feasible simply because of the fragility of Black life in a White racist society that is so hostile to blackness. Clarke, however, speaks to the problematic assumptions of such an argument:

> Homosexuality is viewed as a threat to the continued existence of the heterosexual family, because homosexual unions do not, in and of themselves, produce offspring — as if one's only function within a family, within a relationship, or in sex were to produce offspring. Black family lifestyles and homosexual lifestyles are not antithetical. Most black lesbians and gay men grew up in families and are still critically involved with their families. Many black lesbians and gay men are raising children. Why must the black family be so strictly viewed as the result of a heterosexual dyad?[26]

Audre Lorde also denounces the connection between homosexuality and Black genocide:

> At a recent Black literary conference, a heterosexual Black woman stated that to endorse lesbianism was to endorse the death of our race. This position reflects acute fright or a faulty reasoning.... This position supposes that if we do not eradicate lesbianism in the Black community, all Black women will become lesbians. It also supposes that lesbians do not have children. Both suppositions are patently false.[27]

Despite the falsity of these types of claims, Black thinkers have made them with relative impunity. For instance, Black sociologists Nathan and Julia Hare argued in their 1984 book, *The Endangered Black Family: Coping with the Unisexualization and Coming Extinction of the Black Race,* that homosexuality was a sign of "family disintegration" and a "decaying and decadent society." The Hares presume that "homosexuality does not promote black family stability and that it historically has been a product largely of the Europeanized society."[28]

Black female ethicist Cheryl Sanders places a "sacred canopy" over such rhetoric. In arguing against the use of a womanist nomenclature by Christian religious scholars, since a womanist stance implies an acceptance of gay and lesbian sexuality, Sanders says:

> In my view there is a discrepancy between the womanist criteria that would affirm and/or advocate homosexual practice, and the ethical norms the black church might employ to promote the survival and wholeness of black families. It is problematic for those of us who claim connectedness to and concern for the black family

and church to engage these criteria authoritatively and/or uncritically in the formulation of theological-ethical discourse for those two institutions. If black women's ethics is to be pertinent to the needs of our community, then at least some of us must be in a position to offer intellectual guidance to the church as the principal (and perhaps only remaining) advocate for marriage and family in the black community. There is a great need for the black churches to promote a positive sexual ethics within the black community as one means of responding to the growing normalization of a single-parent family, and the attendant increases in poverty, welfare dependency, and a host of other problems. Moreover, it is indisputably in the best interest of black children for the church not only to strengthen and support existing families, but also to educate them ethically for marriage and parenthood.[29]

Homosexuality: A Threat to Black Manhood

Even as homosexuality is seen as a threat to Black families, Black families have been held responsible for causing homosexuality, especially among males. Following the logic of the Moynihan Report, many Black homophobic arguments stress the importance of a male-dominated family model. They suggest that the absence of such a model leaves young Black males woefully susceptible to the "disease" of homosexuality. This argument, which is an indirect accusation against the Black woman, is based on the false assumption that male homosexuality is equated with effeminate behavior. In the minds of various Black thinkers, homosexuality indicates a defect in the development of Black masculinity and is a perversion of manhood. Jawanza Kunjufu argues, for example, that young males who do not experience enough male companionship are "prime candidates for homosexuality."[30] Asante sharpens this perspective:

> The rise of homosexuality in the African-American male's psyche is real and complicated. An Afrocentric perspective recognizes its existence but homosexuality cannot be condoned or accepted as good for the national development of a strong people. It can be and must be tolerated until such time as our families and schools are engaged in Afrocentric instructions for males.... The time has come for us to redeem our manhood through planned Afrocentric action.[31]

Again reflective of patriarchal/sexist norms, manhood in the Black community is inextricably related to physical strength, independence, and dominance. Given such a notion, nowhere does the image of manhood, and the desire to protect it, come into more conflict with homosexuality than in the world of sports. The Black athlete is portrayed as the quintessence of masculinity. It is therefore no surprise that anything that would impugn the "manhood" of the Black male athlete is quickly dismissed or denied. Such is the case with homosexuality.

While the shared kiss between Isaiah Thomas and Magic Johnson prior to the 1988 NBA championship games was acceptable as a part of the on-court rituals of male bonding, that Magic Johnson contracted HIV was not all right. Because the disease was so wrongly associated with gay men, the world of Black athletes quickly disassociated itself from Magic by voicing unwarranted fear over becoming infected by him and by creating an image of Black athletes as heterosexual family men. The players often made references to their wives or to their need to rethink their promiscuous heterosexual behavior. As for Magic Johnson, he quickly and fervently denounced any speculation that he may be gay. Shortly after his announcement that he was HIV positive, he appeared on the *Arsenio Hall Show* and proclaimed that "I'm far from being homosexual." He followed this announcement with assurances that he was infected as a result of unprotected sex with a woman. As if to eradicate any lingering doubt concerning his sexuality (meaning his masculinity), Magic made very public his extremely promiscuous heterosexual lifestyle. It seemed to matter more to him that the public knew he was a "man" than to protect his wife from humiliating references to his lack of fidelity during their long courtship. As if to cement his "manly" sexuality, Magic also made not-too-subtle references in public interviews to the fact that despite his HIV infection he and his wife still enjoyed an active sex life.

Finally, it cannot be overemphasized that Black sexism is clearly manifest in this protection of masculinity and manhood. As seen earlier, homosexuality is often wrongly associated with effeminate behaviors. It is no surprise then that the strong Black mother is blamed for creating the gay male. But nowhere does the sexism of homophobia make itself more manifest than in the responses to lesbians.

The Lesbian Threat

Lesbians are often thought of as a betrayal of manhood by simple virtue of who they are. Malicious references to "dykes" or "bulldaggers" insinuate that they are some deviant form of a wanna-be man. In actuality, there is perhaps no individual perceived as more challenging to male prerogatives than a lesbian. Barbara Christian explains: "By being sexually independent of men, lesbians, by their very existence, call into question society's definition of woman at its deepest levels."[32] Thus, in a society that grants privilege to White heterosexual males, Black lesbians suffer under a tremendous burden within the society at large as well as in the Black community. This is in part due to the fact that the Black man's quest for manhood, according to White patriarchal definitions, is threatened by the presence of Black lesbians. Clarke explains: "The black man may view the lesbian — who cannot be manipulated or seduced sexually by him — in much the same way the white slave master once viewed the black male, viz. as some perverse caricature of manhood threatening his position of dominance over the female body."[33]

Indeed, some Black people's desire to maintain a degree of privilege in a White patriarchal society makes homophobia even more formidable in the Black community. In a society where privilege is accorded on the basis of race (namely, whiteness), gender (maleness), and sexual preference (heterosexuality), heterosexual privilege is virtually the only privilege that Black people — especially Black women — can claim in order to move to the center. In the words of Cheryl Clarke, "heterosexuality was one of [black people's] only means of power over [their] condition as slaves."[34]

Barbara Smith speaks specifically of the heterosexual privilege accorded many Black women: "Heterosexual privilege is usually the only privilege that Black women have. None of us have racial or sexual privilege, almost none of us have class privilege, maintaining 'straightness' is our last resort."[35] Patricia Hill Collins also recognizes this point of privilege:

> In the same way that the white feminists identify with their victimization as women yet ignore the privilege that racism grants them, and that Black men decry racism yet see sexism as less objectionable, African American women may perceive their own race and gender oppression, yet victimize someone else by invoking the benefits of heterosexual privilege.[36]

Collins further points out that homophobic stances, like silence, also shield Black women from becoming a part of the "ultimate other" in relation to the heterosexual White male norm upheld by White culture.

Silence ostensibly protects them from being labeled as lesbians. Collins clarifies, "For Black women who have already been labeled the other by virtue of our race and gender, the threat of being labeled a lesbian can have a chilling effect on Black women's ideas and on our relationships with one another."[37] Karen Baker-Fletcher admits that a fear of being "labeled" or ostracized is perhaps a significant factor in womanist theological silence surrounding issues of homophobia. She says of womanist silence, "I suspect that for many it is for the same reason that many gays and lesbians hesitate to come out of the closet: fear of losing a job, of being thrown out of church, ostracized in community."[38]

It has also been pointed out, and rightly so, that many Black women are rendered silent or are even vocal homophobes because of their fears concerning their own feelings for women. Audre Lorde recognizes this when she says, "[T]he Black lesbian is an emotional threat only to those Black women whose feelings of kinship and love for other Black women are problematic in some way."[39] Barbara Smith pointedly says, "I think the reason that Black women are so homophobic is the attraction-repulsion thing. They have to speak out vociferously against lesbianism because if they don't they may have to deal with their own deep feelings for women."[40]

So what does all of this mean in the Black community? The first general conclusion to be drawn is that the discussion of homosexuality in the Black community is not a simple matter. Homophobia does not reflect merely a close-minded sexual bigotry by Black men and women. This is a phobia and prejudice nurtured in large part by a history of White sexual exploitation. The case supporting homophobia in the Black community reveals homophobia almost as a misguided strategy for protecting Black lives and the integrity of Black sexuality, as a necessary position to safeguard Black life and freedom. Homosexuality is seen as threatening Black well-being. The passion that often surrounds homophobic attitudes is perhaps best understood in light of Black people's mistaken efforts to protect "authentic blackness" rather than as a sign of a community more intensely homophobic than other communities.

Yet while appreciating the history of oppression that shapes Black homophobia certainly makes it easier to understand the intransigence of homophobia in the Black community, it does not make it any more acceptable. Black homophobia cannot be excused. Regardless of the reasons for it, it is wrong because it negates the unique richness, value, and worth of human beings. As Cheryl Clarke rightly puts it, "[black people] cannot rationalize the disease of homophobia among

black people as the white man's fault, for to do so is to absolve ourselves of our responsibility to transform ourselves."[41] How can this
transformation begin?

HOMOPHOBIA AND A SEXUAL DISCOURSE
OF RESISTANCE

Such transformation cannot take place apart from a sexual discourse
of resistance. This discourse is the first step toward helping Black men
and women to understand that homophobia threatens Black well-being
instead of protecting it. A discourse of resistance must expose how the
sexual politics of White culture, with its varied attacks on Black sexuality, has made it appear that homophobia is compatible with Black
life and freedom, even though this is not so. By exposing the relationships among race, sex, and power, a discourse of resistance will show
that homophobia plays into the hands of White culture and racism.
Homophobia does this by creating discord among Black people. Audre
Lorde would no doubt describe Black homophobia as "horizontal hos-
tility" because it causes Black people to fight one another instead of the
structures of oppression that truly threaten Black life.[42]

And what is most significant, homophobia destroys Black life because it impairs the Black community's ability to respond to HIV/AIDS,
a disease that has devastated the Black community. Though Black
people constitute only 12 to 13 percent of the U.S. population, they
account for at least 57 percent of all HIV/AIDS cases. Regardless of
the disproportionate numbers of Black people affected by HIV/AIDS,
the Black community has been slow in responding to this illness. As
pointed out earlier, clearly one of the reasons for such a slow response
has been the homophobic association of this illness with homosexuality.
Homophobia mimics White culture in the way it destroys Black lives.
Keith Boykin says it incisively:

> With all the efforts being made to divide minorities, it is impor-
> tant to remember that the real enemy is injustice, not each other.
> Homophobia, not homosexuality, leads some lesbians and gays
> to engage in risky and self-destructive behaviors. Homophobia,
> not homosexuality, leads many of them away from their families,
> their communities and their places of worship. And when clos-
> eted black lesbians and gays continue to deceive themselves with
> unsuccessful marriages and families, it is homophobia, not homo-

sexuality, that threatens the survival of the African-American family.

The enemy within us is often more threatening than the enemies surrounding us. But that internal enemy is not homo-sexuality but, rather, the hurtful way we treat one another. Physically, spiritually, and intellectually, blacks are warring against each other instead of supporting each other.[43]

It is perhaps in revealing that homophobia is actually *contrary* to the well-being of Black life that Black people might arrive at a more liberat-ing view of the biblical tradition in matters of sexuality. It might allow the Black community to lift the sacred canopy that it has placed over homophobia. To reiterate, the authority of scripture is in large measure determined by whether or not a text supports the life and freedom of the Black community. A sexual discourse of resistance should clarify that homophobia is antithetical to Black life and freedom and thus dis-rupt the terrorizing manner in which Black people have used biblical texts in regard to homosexuality.

Finally, a sexual discourse of resistance should help Black people understand how they are using the very tools of power that have been used against them to oppress gay and lesbian persons. They take up these tools when they construct sexual discourse against gay and les-bian persons and shelter it under a biblical sacred canopy, suggesting that such sexuality is an abomination to God and that it endangers Black existence. This discourse serves to denigrate and destroy a signif-icant segment of Black humanity, in much the same way that White sexual discourse seeks to destroy Black people.

The Black community's sexual discourse against homosexuality does not save Black lives, but rather helps White culture to destroy them. In this regard Lorde is right: "The master's tools will never dismantle the master's house."[44] A discourse of resistance will stress that Black well-being is *not* fostered by adopting the oppressive, destructive, life-negating tools of White culture. The community must be constrained in its dialogue and action by its concern for the flourishing of Black life. A sexual discourse of resistance could nurture the kind of discussion that promotes acceptance and appreciation of the rich diversity — even sexual diversity — within the Black community. It would empower, if not compel, Black men and women to disavow and dismantle any struc-tures, systems, or ways of behaving or thinking that in any way foster homophobia.

CONCLUSIONS

This chapter has shown the significance of a sexual discourse of resistance for the Black community. Without such a discourse homophobia can exist with relative impunity because it masquerades as a defender of Black life and freedom. At the same time a sacred canopy remains intact and serves as a divine affirmation of Black homophobia. A sexual discourse of resistance may help to dismantle this homophobic sacred canopy by exposing the links between the exploitation of Black sexuality and the intensity of Black homophobia. Ultimately, it will reveal that homophobia actually betrays Black self-interest and Black life.

In the end, what does this discussion of sexuality have to do with theology, more specifically with the Black theological tradition? While the ability to foster and nurture Black life and wholeness is a compelling enough reason for theologians, especially womanist theologians, to engage in sexual discourse, there are even more compelling reasons for doing so. As we will discover, the core belief of Black faith in a God who came down to earth in Jesus Christ demands a sexual discourse of resistance.

PART 3

A THEOLOGY OF BLACK SEXUALITY

CHAPTER 5

God-Talk and Black Sexuality

Refrains like "O when I talk I talk with God," "Massa Jesus is my bosom friend," "He will be wid us Jesus / Be wid us to the end," "A little talk wid Jesus makes it right," "I'm goin' to talk with [live with, see] King Jesus by myself, by myself," and "He's King of Kings, and Lord of Lords / Jesus Christ, the first and the last / No man works like him" have echoed through the songs of the enslaved. These songs reveal a people's faith in a God who is neither abstract nor remote, but one who is intimate and personal. The enslaved testified in song and word to a God who through Jesus comes down to earth and is made real as friend, confidant, healer, and liberator.

Though the enslaved crafters of the Black faith tradition did not refer to Jesus in the theological jargon of dominant Western culture as the "word made flesh," as the divine/human encounter, or as the incarnate one, they did witness in a clear-cut, theologically incisive manner to the radical uniqueness of Jesus and the oneness between Jesus and God. In their own ordinary, everyday manner the enslaved testified to a God whose self-disclosure in Jesus Christ revealed that God was present in human history, in their history, as one who cared about their life and freedom. Such testimony was significant as it revealed the enslaved's rejection of the slaveholders' understanding of God as one who supported and sanctioned cruel, inhumane enslavement. God's radical embodied revelation was thus a central theme in the faith of the enslaved that persists in the faith of Black churchpeople today.

Reminiscent of the songs of their foreparents, Black churchpeople continue to witness to the immediate, intimate, living presence of a God made manifest in Jesus Christ. They sing the gospel songs "I Had a Talk with Jesus," "I Know God," "I Want Jesus to Walk with Me," and "Jesus Is Real to Me."

While enslaved Black people nurtured a theology based on belief in a just God who was actively and intimately present in their history, they also fostered the notion of being created in the image of this God. In the language of their own experience and using the Old Testament imagery of being a chosen people, enslaved men and women testified in song that they too were children of God, created in God's own image. Spirituals were filled with lyrics like these: "We are the people of God"; "We are de people of de Lord"; "I really do believe I'm a child of God." Such testimony was quite revolutionary because it was a denial of White slaveholders' claims that blackness was an affront to God and that Black people were *not* children of God. Black Christians still carry forth this radical affirmation of their intrinsic connection to God as they sing a song like, "I got a robe, you got a robe, *all* of God's children got a robe."

Central to the faith of Black churchpeople, a legacy from the religion of the enslaved, is the attestation of Jesus as Christ, the embodied presence of God, and the avowal that Black people are created in God's own image. These two theological confessions suggest the centrality of sexuality to the Black Christian faith. To corrupt, misconstrue, deny, or simply ignore Black sexuality is a betrayal of Christianity in general and Black faith in particular, especially since these stances portend a distorted understanding of and diminished relationship with God. Now, we will look more closely at what it means to be created in the image of the God disclosed in Jesus and at the intrinsic relationship between sexuality and Christianity, with special attention given to Black faith.

CREATED IN THE IMAGE OF THE GOD
OF JESUS CHRIST

Any appreciation for what it means to be created in the image of God and to reflect that image must begin with what makes Christianity distinctive, God's self-disclosure in Jesus. The Christian faith is organized around the belief that Jesus, the first-century Jew from Nazareth, is the "word made flesh," the embodied presence of God. Christians believe that through Jesus, God is perfectly revealed.

Notwithstanding the historically dominant tradition of the church that demonizes the flesh, the claim that God has become incarnate has made at least two things clear. First, God's embodied presence in Jesus affirms the testimony of the first chapter of Genesis that all of God's creation was good, including the human body. In view of the stated "goodness" of creation, God's revelation in Jesus should have precluded Christians from accepting Platonic or Gnostic notions that reviled the human body/flesh. Jesus Christ, the incarnate one, suggests the inherent contradiction between Christianity and any form of spiritualistic dualism that tends to place the soul and body in an innately antagonistic relationship. The message of God's embodiment in Jesus is unambiguous: the human body is not a cauldron of evil but, rather, an instrumentality for divine presence. It is the medium by which God is made "real" to humanity, through which God interacts in human history. To accept that Jesus, the first-century Jew from Nazareth, is God incarnate indicates that in Jesus divinity and humanity are irrevocably united.

Even though the way divinity and humanity are "unconfusedly, unalterably, undividedly, and inseparably" united (the language of Chalcedon) has been both a mystery and a scandal for the church, it has nonetheless been the church's chief confession since Nicaea (325) and Chalcedon (451) that in Jesus there is a perfect union of both divinity and humanity. Those who would argue that Jesus was not fully human or that his humanity corrupted his divinity were defeated at those councils. Again, Jesus as the complete revelation of God discloses the compatibility between humanity and divinity as the two are perfectly united.

This divine/human union leads us to the second message of God's embodied presence: God is present with us through our very humanity. Twentieth-century German theologian Karl Barth's description of Jesus helps to explicate this point. Barth calls Jesus Christ the "humanity of God."[1] To him, Jesus, God's perfect presence in human history, signifies that God's love for humanity was so strong that God came to humanity. Since humanity was incapable on its own of going to God, God was moved to reach out to humanity, according to Barth, strictly out of love. Thus, the very humanity of God is seen through the outpouring of God's love, which is God's reaching out to be in particular relationship with humanity. (More will be said about the particularity of this relationship in our discussion of Jesus.)

By recognizing God's embodied presence in Jesus as the "humanity of God," Barth, whether he intended to or not, insinuates the very meaning of authentic humanity. Such authenticity is found in a divine love for humanity that inspires human beings to also give of themselves in loving relationships. A person's humanity is actualized when he or she, motivated by God's love, enters into a relationship with the rest of God's creation. To know the love of God is to be compelled to share that love with others. To do so is also to realize one's own divinity. As

Jesus Christ attests to the essential relationship between his humanity and divinity, likewise our authentic humanity is essentially related to the realization of our relationship to the divine. To manifest our loving relationship to God is to be in a loving relationship with God's creation. This is a fundamental aspect of what it means to be created in the image of God.

Women and men who choose to reflect the *imago Dei* in the world are agents of loving relationships with God's creation. The writer of 1 John puts it this way: "Beloved, let us love one another, because love is from God; everyone who loves is born of God and knows God. Whoever does not love does not know God because God is love. . . . God is love, and those who abide in love abide in God, and God abides in them" (1 John 4:7–8, 16b).

It must also be understood that though women and men are loved by God, it is not inevitable that they will share in that love. That God loves every single human being is certain, but that every single human being will manifest that love is not certain. Because God's love abides in every human being by virtue of God's entering into relationship with humanity, every human being is created in the image of God. But there is no assurance that every human being will manifest that divine image. To do so requires that individuals freely choose to share the love of God as God freely chose to love them. This is made plain in 1 John 4: "Those who say, 'I love God,' and hate their brothers or sisters, are liars; for those who do not love a brother or sister whom they have seen, cannot love God whom they have not seen. The commandment we have from him is this: those who love God must love their brothers and sisters also" (1 John 4:20–21).

Carter Heyward puts it succinctly: "Our love of humanity is our love of God; and our love of God is our love of humanity."[2] To reiterate, to love God and thus to love humanity is to live out a fundamental aspect of what it means to be created in God's own image. The life and ministry of Jesus make all of this even more explicit.

Who Jesus was as God's embodied presence, though not fully captured by his ministry, was certainly inseparable from his ministry. The Gospel of Luke makes the connection explicit in Luke's recording of Jesus' first public sermon:

> The Spirit of the Lord is upon me,
>   because he has anointed me
>   to bring good news to the poor.

> He has sent me to proclaim release to the captives
>> and recovery of sight to the blind,
>>> to let the oppressed go free,
> to proclaim the year of the Lord's favor. (Luke 4:18–19)

What Jesus did — his ministry — reveals his divinity and what it means to share the love of God. His ministry was characterized by giving of himself to others so that they might experience justice, healing, belonging, self-worth, life, and/or empowerment. This meant that at times Jesus castigated the unjust, cured physical ailments or infirmities (made the blind to see, the lame to walk), established relationships with outcasts (the lepers, the woman at the well), and raised the dead (Lazarus, Jairus's daughter). Essentially, Jesus was decidedly partial to justice and to those who were victims of any form of oppression. He did not tolerate hate, prejudice of any kind, or the marginalizing of people because of their physical, social, or economic condition, and neither did he tolerate neutrality in the face of human misery or injustice. Consistently and in various ways, Jesus instructed his followers that if a person was hungry, sick, homeless, naked, or in need in some other way, then they must attempt to meet that need.

The love of God made manifest in Jesus is what has come to be understood as agape. Agape is God's love. It is an active love, the giving of oneself for the sake of justice and the building of an authentically human (loving) community. By perfectly manifesting agape, Jesus' life and ministry, as the presence of God in the world, reinforce the understanding that to reflect the image of God is to do nothing less than nurture loving relationships. This, then, brings us to human sexuality.

A positive embrace of human sexuality is critical to agape, and it is crucial for those who would radiate what it means to be created in the image of God. Human sexuality *is* what provides men and women with the capacity to enter into relationships with others. Sexuality is that dimension of humanity that urges relationship. Sexuality is a gift from God that, if properly appreciated, helps women and men to become more fully human by entering into loving relationships. "Sexuality thus expresses God's intention that we find our authentic humanness in relationship."[3]

Before looking at further ramifications of what it means to live in the image of God and the consequent challenges for Black sexuality, let us be more explicit about the general theological implications of what has been said so far.

A Disembodied View of the Incarnation

The view of God's revelation in Jesus Christ that stresses embodiment makes a definite break with theological perspectives that imply that Jesus Christ was a unique metaphysical or mystical union between God and humanity. Such perspectives fall perilously close to Docetism, a denial of the full humanity of Jesus. By emphasizing a metaphysical or mystical union while virtually ignoring God's embodiment, these views depreciate the human body. They insinuate that though God was revealed in Jesus, the embodiment was only incidental to the actual divine revelation in Jesus. They do not take seriously the radical meaning of the incarnation, that God was in fact *en sarki* (in the flesh). Such views, perhaps best described as *disembodied interpretations* of the incarnation, fail to do several things.

First, they do not take seriously the contextuality of God's revelation. Disembodied understandings do not indicate an awareness that just as the revelation of God reveals something about the context into which God enters, so too the context reveals something about God. The context itself is revelatory. That is, the God of Jesus Christ is one whose radical disclosure is best understood from the vantage point of the marginalized, outcast, and oppressed in society. The Black enslaved witnessed to this fact as they sang, "Poor little Jesus Boy / Born in a manger / World treat him mean / Treat me mean too." As we shall see later, to take seriously the context of God's revelation in Jesus clearly has direct implications for how gay and lesbian persons are viewed in church and society.

Second, such disembodied interpretations do not take seriously that it was through the very body of Jesus that God's humanity was expressed. Through his body Jesus was able to interact in the world and to enter into relationship with others. Moreover, that Jesus touched, healed, and raised the dead indicates his own respect for the bodies of others. The body can be a vehicle for divine presence and the means by which human beings can communicate agape. The body is the physicality of sexuality, that which signals the potential for one to be authentically human and hence to reflect the image of God in the world. A disembodied approach to God's disclosure in Jesus subverts the very radicality of God's disclosure. It negates the significance of God's presence in human history by metaphysicalizing and mystifying God's revelation in Jesus.

Correspondingly, by neglecting the embodied God, this approach renders the life and ministry of Jesus inconsequential. The Nicaea/ Chalcedon confession is in this respect a quintessential example of such a disembodied interpretation of the incarnation. The formulation reads:

> We believe in one God, Father, Ruler of all, Maker of heaven and earth.... And in one Lord Jesus Christ, the only-begotten Son of God, begotten from the Father before all ages..., who for us human beings and for our salvation came down from heaven and was incarnate from the Holy Spirit and Mary the Virgin and became human; and was crucified for us under Pontius Pilate, and suffered, and was buried, and rose on the third day in accordance with the Scriptures.

By moving directly from the incarnation to the crucifixion and resurrection, this confession nullifies the importance of embodiment to God's revelation. The implication is that what took place between Jesus' birth and resurrection is unimportant to what it meant for him to be Christ. This confession suggests that who Jesus was as the incarnate one was not related to his life and ministry. His very embodiment, then, becomes little more than an accident of God's entrance into history through him. Ironically, while the Nicaea/Chalcedon confession defeated Docetic-like claims that denied the full humanity of Jesus, it did so most inadequately. It maintained a spiritualistic dualism by devaluing the ministry of Jesus and hence rendering the body extraneous to the incarnation itself. The Nicaea/Chalcedon confession thus left room for Christians to construe the human body as an impediment to divinity.

An Embodied View of the Incarnation

So, paradoxically, while the enslaved were deprived of access to Western theological traditions and jargon, they already possessed a most penetrating and accurate view of the incarnation. By witnessing to God's presence in human history through God's reality in their daily lives and by utilizing a language that emerged from their everyday lives of struggle, the enslaved maintained the integrity of God's disclosure in Jesus. Their testimony of Jesus as one who understood their tears and pain, as one who walked with them, talked with them, and understood their grief affirmed that Jesus was a real historical presence who brought God to earth. The enslaved testimony clarified what the Nicaea/Chalcedon councils attempted to declare: that in Jesus, God was actually *en sarki,* incarnate, an embodied reality in human history.

A fundamental theological task of the Black Christian community becomes clear. This task is to follow in the tradition of the enslaved community of faith and to disavow disembodied interpretations of the incarnation by pointing to God's concrete existence. In so doing, a sexual discourse of resistance must emerge that heeds the testimony of ordinary men and women who struggle daily for survival and freedom. Their witness to God's reality in their lives is a critical resource for penetrating the meaning of the incarnation, even as it reminds us that the best vantage point from which to perceive the fundamental significance of the incarnation is that of the marginalized, those whom the "world also treats mean."

Such testimony also continually reminds us that God is made known to us through God's embodied actions in human history. We are challenged to demystify incarnation-talk by diligently explicating the ways that God is actualized in the lives of people, as healer, listener, empowerer, liberator, and so on. To reiterate, the incarnation indicates that God is embodied in human history through Jesus Christ and, as such, is an intimately active presence in the lives of women and men. A sexual discourse of resistance seeks to protect this historical realness of God's revelation in Jesus.

Such a view demands a theological understanding of the body. It does not compel an idolatrous worship of the body, but it does compel an appreciation of the body as indeed "the very temple of God," as the medium of God's love. It is by becoming embodied that God was distinctly revealed in human history; moreover, it is only via bodies that human beings can come to know and be in relationship with one another. We reach out to one another with our bodies, and we accept one another as embodied.

Such a view values Jesus' life and ministry, and it also implies that what took place through the person of Jesus is available to ordinary men and women. To be like Jesus does not necessitate some mysterious, metaphysical action by God. Rather, it requires living a life characterized by loving relationships, those that are liberating, healing, empowering, and life-sustaining. In this regard, the uniqueness of Jesus is related not to his simply being the embodied presence of God, but to his *perfection* as that embodied presence. What Jesus achieved perfectly, humans can achieve less perfectly. Carter Heyward makes a similar point: "If we are as fully human as we are able to be, and Jesus suggested we *are* able to be, then we are godders, we god — human beings/created bodies bringing God to life again, and again."[4]

•

Finally, as an embodied interpretation of God's disclosure in Jesus clarifies that the divinity of God is intrinsically related to the humanity of God, it also suggests that this God of Jesus Christ is in essence relational. In this regard, the doctrine of the Trinity points to something crucial about the very nature of God. Despite the sexist manner in which the doctrine has been expressed (Father, Son, and Holy Ghost) and even its inherent confusion, the Trinitarian doctrine avows a God who is internally and eternally relational. God in Godself, the Godhead, is in a relationship of mutuality and reciprocity as creator, redeemer, and sustainer. Such a God, as the incarnation avers, is best known in human history by way of an equivalent loving relationship with humanity. Heyward again makes a poignantly similar point: "[T]here is an important impulse behind the [Trinitarian] doctrine. An important dimension of human intuition. An intuition of ultimacy in relation. An intuition of a God who is 'internally' relational."[5]

To summarize, God's self-disclosure in Jesus exposes what the Trinitarian formula actually expresses — God is intrinsically relational. Therefore, being created in and reflecting the image of God have meaning only to the degree to which human beings are in relationships governed by love. One other dimension of the image of God expressed in the Trinitarian doctrine, God as creator, also affirms the divine purpose of human sexuality.

The Passion of God

God's love is revealed as nothing else if not life-generating energy. God is creator. God grants life. It is God's commitment to life that evinces the passion of God. The Gospel of John captures this divine passion: "God so loved the world that God gave his only begotten Son so that all who believe may not perish, but have eternal life" (John 3:16). The giving up of Jesus on the cross reveals God's passion, the lengths to which God will suffer to foster life. The passion of God, therefore, reflects two aspects of the word "passion."

"Passion" — as derived from the Latin term *passio* — refers to suffering, and it also refers to a powerful emotion, such as ardent love. In this regard, God's passion reveals the inextricable connection between God's suffering and God's love of life. God is willing to suffer for God's ardent love of life. Unless one appreciates that God's passion signals love as well as suffering, then the passion of God can too easily be interpreted as suggesting the necessity of redemptive suffering in order to be more like God, that is, in order to reflect God's presence in the world. God's passion is not about the need to suffer. Instead, it is about the love of life. Again, God's passion attests to God's ardent commitment to life and hence God's willingness to suffer so that life might flourish. Such an understanding of God's passion has strong implications for what it means to reflect the image of God and thus, again, calls up the question of sexuality.

God's passion suggests a broader understanding of human passion. Human passion must be seen as more than lust or desire for sexual activity. Audre Lorde, for instance, describes it as an "erotic" force. She says, "[I]t is an assertion of the lifeforce of women; of that creative energy empowered."[6] Baptist minister Patricia Hunter calls passion "unquenchable thirst for that which is not yet. Passion is that determined desire to know ourselves and others completely. Passion is our souls' desire for harmony born of justice."[7]

Heyward defines it as

a way of being in which anything less than spilling over with the Spirit of God is not enough; spilling over with desire to know and do the will of God in our daily work and play; with righteous and active indignation at injustice, with careful caring for others and self, with courage to stand up and be counted — when it counts; spilling over with integrity in relationship with awareness of our oneness with all aspects and persons of creation.[8]

For me, passion encompasses all that is said in the above definitions. It is that divine energy within human beings, the love of God, that compels them toward life-giving, life-producing, and life-affirming activity and relationships in regard to all of God's creation. So while passion certainly encompasses the biological production of life, it means more than that. It is a powerful, creative dynamism. It is a glimpse of God's perfect passion for life. Human passion is God's passion bursting forth from the human being as an insatiable desire to foster life in all aspects of one's living. Such an understanding and appreciation for human passion as a glimpse of God's own passion demand an embrace of human sexuality.

While sexuality and passion are not synonymous, they are inextricably linked. Human sexuality is a vehicle through which one's passion is expressed. It is a receptacle for passion. It is a means by which humans can share in God's intense love for life. It is a central factor in recognizing the human role in God's ongoing creative activity.

Once again, then, human sexuality must be viewed as a gift from God. It is not, as spiritualistic dualism suggests, a human flaw. Rather, it is significant to the human capacity to show forth the image of God. Sexuality allows human beings to be in loving relationships that are inevitably life-affirming and life-producing. Women and men must then be able to celebrate, affirm, and experience their sexuality fully in order to know and experience who they are as children of God created in God's own image. Anything less than a positive acceptance of human sexuality heralds a faulty conception of what it means to be created in the image of the God revealed in Jesus Christ. Let us now explore what this suggests concerning theological imperatives for a Black sexual discourse of resistance.

SEXUAL DISCOURSE
AND AUTHENTIC BLACK FAITH

It is important for Black and womanist theologians to engage in and promote a sexual discourse of resistance not only because of the need to restore the relationship between human sexuality and the God of Jesus Christ, but also to connect Black faith back with its "authentic" religious heritage and to liberate Black people from the cycle of White cultural sin.

When Black churchpeople approach human sexuality as a vessel of sin and evil — as they perceive it to be only about genitals and sexual activity and as they refuse to promote frank public discourse concerning sexuality — they betray their enslaved religious heritage in that they have adopted the dominant Western European and Euro-American tradition of spiritualistic dualism and pietism. Recent interpreters of the religion of the enslaved have concluded that the African religious heritage significantly shaped enslaved Africans' interpretation of Christianity. Black religious scholars variously argue that the enslaved used their African worldview, culture, and religious heritage "to make Christianity their own."

The African cosmological understanding in which there was no distinction between sacred and secular reality had a profound impact on the religious and spiritual views of the enslaved. As chapter 3 pointed out, "secularity has no life in many African traditions."[9] This means that there is no diminution of the earthly realm, that is, things of the flesh. Every dimension of the world and humanity, according to numerous African religions, is spiritual, is of God, and communicates God's presence. It is no wonder, then, that the enslaved were able to give witness to God by emphasizing God's very humanity. They testified in word and song that God was real because of God's relationship with them made manifest through Jesus Christ. No doubt because the enslaved inherited and maintained an African religious tradition in which things of the flesh were not associated with evil, they could fully appreciate the humanity of God, hence the fullness of God's revelation in Jesus. The enslaved Africans saw no contradiction between flesh and divinity. There was little temptation, therefore, to follow the tradition of their slaveholders, the legacy of Nicaea, which projected a disembodied view of the incarnation. They joyously testified to a God who feeds the hungry, clothes the poor, and heals the sick as well as a God they could talk to and laugh with.

In this regard, one can say that the religion of the enslaved bore witness to the true meaning of Christianity in the way it maintained the integrity of the radical meaning of Jesus Christ. A disembodied view of the incarnation (especially as it ignores the ministry of Jesus) allows for the compatibility of Christianity and slavery, just as spiritualistic dualism — the progenitor of such a view — spawns sexist and racist views of humanity. An appreciation of God's embodied presence condemns slavery and other forms of human oppression for the way in which they contradict the very presence of God revealed in Jesus Christ.

A sexual discourse of resistance is necessary to call Black people back to their African religious heritage, which rightly views human sexuality as divine. Such a discourse will make it abundantly clear that, on the one hand, an African perspective has fostered an understanding of Christianity that supports the quest for Black life and wholeness, while, on the other hand, a Euro-American, "flesh-denying" perspective has fostered Black oppression, especially the denigration and exploitation of Black sexuality. A Black sexual discourse of resistance, while clarifying the meaning of God's revelation in Jesus, will basically highlight the life-sustaining and liberative strands of Black faith grounded in a religious tradition, at once African and Christian, that affirms the goodness of human sexuality in all of its complexity.

Sexual Discourse and the Cycle of Sin

There is another reason that Black and womanist theologies are obligated to advocate a sexual discourse, and that is to break the cycle of sin created by the White cultural exploitation of Black sexuality. White cultural attacks upon Black sexuality are inherently sinful because they alienate persons from their bodies and their sexuality and, hence, from God. Such attacks thwart Black self-love and the capacity for Black people to form loving relationships with others. They frustrate Black people's capacity to reflect what it means for them to be created in the image of God.

As mentioned in the previous chapter, White cultural attacks have infringed upon Black women's and men's appreciation for their own embodied Black selves. White culture has systematically and unrelentingly cast aspersions upon Black physiognomy: hair, skin color, facial features, genitals. This culture has decried blackness as ugly and evil. Unfortunately, too many Black men and women have internalized this profane sexual discourse of White culture. In so doing, they have been unable to authentically love their own bodies. So while Black people may verbalize their love of God, their lack of self-love suggests otherwise. A love of one's own body is a fundamental component to saying a loud yes to God's profound and gracious (meaning, freely given) love.

The radicality of God's love expressed in Jesus Christ means that God loves our very bodies. Jesus Christ clearly signifies that God loves us not in spite of or apart from our bodies, but that God loves us in our bodies as uniquely embodied creatures. Our bodies are the vessels of God's abiding love. To be able to love our own bodies is to be able to accept God's love of us. To be unable to love our bodies is not to know the full measure of God's love. It consequently means that we will not be able to share that love.

In order to respect the bodies and lives of others, we must first respect and love our own bodies and lives. Without self-acceptance, any acceptance of others is virtually impossible. Self-love is the absolute first step to loving others. And, ultimately, if we cannot love others, then we cannot fully love God, as our love for God is manifest through our love of others. In the words of Karen Baker-Fletcher, loving ourselves "is the first order of business" to loving God.[10] The summary of the law referred to in the Bible puts it like this: "You shall love the Lord your God with all your heart, all your soul, and all your mind. You shall love your neighbor as yourself." This commandment clearly shows the interrelatedness of self-love and love of others, as well as the need to love God with *all* that we are as human beings.

Inasmuch as White culture has warped Black people's relationship with themselves and their bodies, it has diminished their valuation of their sexuality. To reiterate, the human body is the physicality of one's sexuality. The consequence of a devalued sexuality is an estranged relationship with God. It cannot be overstated that God is made manifest through loving relationships and that these relationships are made possible because of human sexuality. James Nelson rightly says, "Sexuality ...is intrinsic to our relationship with God."[11] Thus, as Black people are alienated from their bodies, they are alienated from God in two ways: they do not know the profound love of God for them, and they do not know the profound love of God found in loving relationships. Ultimately, then, White culture obfuscates what it means for Black people to reflect the image of God because it impairs their ability for self-love and love of others.

That White culture is sinful is evident. It alienates persons, particularly Black people, from God as it thwarts human relationships. In this regard, both White and Black people potentially participate in the sin of White culture. When a White person remains silent in the face of White culture and reaps the benefits of that culture or nurtures and protects that culture in any way — even by denying its existence — that White person is fortifying his or her own sin. Likewise, the tacit refusal of the Black church and the Black community to engage in sexual discourse signals Black people's complicity in the sin of White culture. Silence in the face of sin is no less than collusion with that sin. Specifically, silence on matters of sexuality leaves Black men and women vulnerable to the spiritual as well as the psychological, emotional, and physical consequences of the White cultural attack upon Black bodies and intimacy.

A sexual discourse of resistance is crucial if the Black community is to break free from the complexity of sin created by the White cultural attack upon Black sexuality. Such a discourse will nurture Black self-love. It will impress upon Black men and women that because of the incarnation the claims of White culture concerning Black bodies are without merit. God's disclosure in Jesus means that God loves Black people in their very blackness. A sexual discourse of resistance will specify that God affirms the "humanity" of blackness. It is through their very Black embodied selves that Black men and women reflect the image of God and that God's love and presence are manifest in the world. In this way, a sexual discourse of resistance will help Black people to recognize that whenever Black men and women love themselves and love others in a human, loving community, then God *is fully* Black and blackness *is fully* God. Blackness is not an affront to

God. It is a fitting existential witness to God's embodied presence in history.

The Sinfulness of White Culture

To label White culture, especially as it exploits Black sexuality, as sin is consistent with previously articulated understandings of sin found in both Black and womanist theologies. James Cone, for example, argues that the essence of God's revelation is God's liberating activity on the side of those who are oppressed. For people to know and be in relationship with this God, according to Cone, requires that they participate in liberating activity on behalf of the oppressed. In addition, Cone suggests that the essence of one's humanity — that is, being in the image of God who is liberator — is bound to participation in liberating activity. Cone explains, "[T]he image [of God] is human nature in rebellion against the structures of oppression. It is humanity involved in the liberation struggle against the forces of inhumanity."[12] Cone then goes on to argue that sin is that which alienates people from their humanity and, hence, from God. According to this liberation paradigm, sin, then, is anything that subverts the liberation process and/or nurtures structures of oppression. When understood in relation to the Black struggle against White racism, Cone names sin as whiteness. He puts it this way:

> The sin of whites is the definition of their existence in terms of whiteness. It is accepting the condition that is responsible for Amerindian reservations, black concentration camps, and the rape of Vietnam. It is believing in the American way of life as defined by its history.[13]

Black people are complicit in the sin of whiteness to the degree that they quest after that which whiteness stands for. Cone says, "[S]in represents the condition of estrangement from the source of one's being, for blacks this means a desire to be white.... Sin, then, for blacks is loss of identity..., [not rebelling] against every infringement of white being on black being."[14]

Drawing upon Black women's historical experience, womanist theologian Delores Williams derives a similar understanding of sin. She argues that sin is that which devalues Black women's humanity and defiles their bodies. This means that "American patriarchy and demonarchy committed against Black women and their children"[15] are sin. It also means that the Black community participates in the sin against Black women inasmuch as it also devalues and defiles their humanity or tolerates structures and systems that do. Black women are also sinful "when they do not challenge the patriarchal and demonarchal systems in society defiling Black women's bodies through physical violence, sexual abuse, and exploited labor."[16] Williams concludes her discussion of sin by delineating four specific features of her "womanist notion of sin." In describing these features, she highlights the importance of the "human body and its sexual resources." More specifically, she designates sin as that which abuses the human body and sexuality: "Sin becomes the disparagement of [Black] women and sexuality and the internalization of the effects of such disparagement in [Black] women's feelings of unworthiness."[17]

To identify sin as racism, sexism, White culture, and cooperation with such tyranny suggests two key points about a Christian perspective on sin and repentance. First, this conception of sin — paralleling in some ways traditional understandings of sin that emphasize individuals who collectively and individually rebel against God — stresses its social character. To the extent that individuals and communities participate in these social sins, they, too, are estranged from God. Thus, there is an individual as well as a communal responsibility for violating the humanity of another and precluding her or him from fully experiencing what it means to be created in the image of God.

Second, repentance thus requires a total conversion for both the individual and community. In terms of the White individual and/or community, repentance necessitates a complete rejection of White culture and an advocacy for that which advances Black life and wholeness. This means, as suggested in chapter 1, a radical dismantling of White culture and the oppressive, White, racist, patriarchal hegemony that it seeks to protect. For Black people, then, repentance requires an affirmation of their own blackness. This means utilizing all of the tools of a Black culture of resistance, expressly a sexual discourse of resistance, to disrupt White culture's hold on Black people, especially their sexuality. It also means resisting any temptation to collude with the powers of White hegemony, even when the temptation is the offer of privilege.

HOMOPHOBIA: A SIN AND BETRAYAL OF BLACK FAITH

A Black sexual discourse of resistance is also constrained to make clear that homophobia and concomitant heterosexist structures and systems (those structures and systems that privilege heterosexuals while discriminating against nonheterosexuals) are sin. In other words, it is not homosexuality but homophobia that is sinful. Just as White cultural exploitation of Black sexuality has impaired Black people's ability to affirm their humanity and what it means to be created in the image of God, so has Black homophobia done the same to numerous gay and lesbian Black persons. Inasmuch as Black gays and lesbians have internalized the venomous rhetoric of homophobia, they have become alienated from God. Furthermore, as the Black church and community espouse sexual rhetoric that castigates gay and lesbian sexuality and/or admonishes gay and lesbian persons for experiencing the fullness of their sexuality, this church and community have again participated in and abetted sin. Even more significantly, if God's revelation in Jesus draws us to hear the voices of those who are most marginalized in our society, then the Black church is certainly drawn to hear the voices of Black gay and lesbian persons as they struggle against the complexity of homophobia/heterosexism.

Given the nature of Black homophobia, as seen in the previous chapter, a Black sexual discourse of resistance must do more than simply label homophobia as sin if it is to achieve Black repentance in regard to homophobia. Drawing parallels between the sin of racism and the sin of homophobia is, no doubt, not enough to provoke conversion. As explained in the previous chapter, some connection must be made between the sin of homophobia and the struggle for Black life and freedom. A Black sexual discourse of resistance must show that homophobia violates "authentic" Black faith — that is, the faith that has sustained Black people in their fight for life and freedom. And, indeed, homophobia does violate the centrality of that faith: God's revelation in Jesus Christ.

If Black and womanist theologies are to fulfill their prophetic theological role, they must engage in a sexual discourse of resistance. This discourse should reveal the basic contradictions between homophobia and the church's belief in a God of justice. At the same time, this discourse should reveal the inconsistency between a belief in the God revealed in Jesus Christ and a spiritualistic/dualistic view of sexuality. Not to engage in and promote a sexual discourse of resistance would be a betrayal of a basic theological task. Yet the mandate for womanist theology is even more precise. The very distinctiveness of a womanist theological perspective dictates engagement in a sexual discourse of resistance.

•

Womanist theology is unique not simply because it reflects what is routinely ignored in theological discourse: the voices of Black women as they struggle to understand God in the midst of their complex life experience. Rather, the uniqueness of womanist thought is captured by one all-encompassing component of Alice Walker's definition of the term "womanist." She writes that a womanist is "committed to survival and wholeness of entire people, male *and* female."[18] Of the many aspects of Walker's four-part definition emphasized by various womanist religious scholars, this aspect is the one that has been unanimously affirmed by these scholars.

In essence, this aspect poignantly reflects Black women's historical experience of being staunchly devoted to the life and well-being of their families and communities, almost to the point of neglecting their own health and welfare. Such loyalty caused a reticence in taking on contemporary "feminist" issues. Many Black women were fearful that an advocacy of feminist concerns might alienate them from Black males and from the joint struggle of Black men and women against White racism. Moreover, the enormity of their commitment to their families and communities has left Black women especially vulnerable to being cast as "Superwomen" who can do it all and survive it all. Nevertheless, Black women have been loyal to family and community, and this loyalty is a component of womanist theology.

Womanist thought is not antagonistic. It emerges from a concern and love for all Black life. It does not mount an attack upon Black men, the Black middle class, or any other segment of the Black community that may enjoy some modicum of privilege within a White patriarchal hegemony. Instead, it is an assault upon the interlocking system and structures of racist, classist, sexist, and heterosexist oppression that serve to divide the community against itself. Womanist theology affirms those understandings of God, Christ, and other aspects of Black faith that promote the life and wholeness of all Black folks while disavowing those that do not.

Another compelling aspect of the womanist commitment to the survival of "entire people" is an appreciation for wholeness. Wholeness refers to at least three interrelated aspects of the Black struggle. First, it implies that an individual is whole, that is, spiritually, emotionally, psychically, and physically healed from the wounds of his/her oppression. Second, wholeness suggests that the Black community is not divided against itself in terms of harboring sexism, classism, colorism, or heterosexism. In other words, the community is free from "horizontal violence." Finally, wholeness means that the community itself is free, liberated from oppression, so that each member of the community can fulfill his/her singular potential as a child of God. It should be noted that wholeness is both a state of being and a state of "be-ing." That is, it is something to be attained perfectly as well as something experienced in the very struggle for wholeness itself. The quest for wholeness thus represents a dynamic process of struggle against whatever would diminish life and freedom.

Because of womanist theology's characteristic commitment to the "wholeness" of the *entire* Black community, it is unarguably constrained to advance a sexual discourse of resistance. As has been shown throughout this text, the degradation of Black sexuality has violently corrupted Black women's and men's attainment of wholeness. Virtually every aspect of Black wholeness has been fractured by the White cultural attack on Black sexuality. Black men and women bear the scars of their sexual humiliation as attempts at self-love are so often frustrated and transformed into a self-hate that leads to life-negating behaviors — homicide, suicide, and risky sex.

Moreover, the consequences of sexual humiliation have left Black men and women vulnerable to adopting perceptions of masculinity and femininity that place them in dysfunctional relationships with each other and oblige them to negate the humanity and worth of gay and lesbian persons whose ways of being challenge their distorted views of sexuality. If womanist theology is not to fall woefully short of its own commitment to wholeness for the entire Black community, it is bound to engage in a sexual discourse of resistance that attempts to unmask the sexual politics of White culture and its impact on the sexual politics of the Black church and community.

By helping Black people to affirm their very sexuality, womanist thought cultivates their potential for living out the *imago Dei* of the incarnate God, that is, being in a loving relationship with themselves and with the rest of God's creation. Only as dynamic, existential examples of the *imago Dei* can Black people achieve authentic wholeness. Such an achievement will signal the end of homophobia or any other horizontal violence or tyranny that prevents other human beings from experiencing the fullness of their humanity or from reflecting their divinity.

The first component of Walker's definition describes a womanist displaying "outrageous, audacious, courageous or *willful* behavior." It is time for womanist theologians to live out the meaning of the word "womanist," that is, to outrageously, audaciously, and courageously impress upon the Black church and community the need for a sexual discourse of resistance by willfully engaging in such discourse. To do anything less than this breaks faith with the incarnate God of the Black Christian tradition and dishonors the very core of the womanist idea and ideal.

CONCLUSIONS

This chapter has shown how any authentic Christian theology is constrained to engage in sexual discourse. The center of Christian faith, the God revealed in Jesus Christ, demands an appreciation of human sexuality. As has been argued, human sexuality is a meeting point of the human and divine. It makes it possible for human beings to live out the meaning of being created in the image of God. In addition, the unique perceptiveness of an African-inspired Black faith has maintained the sacredness of human sexuality and thus allowed enslaved Africans to fully grasp the radical implications of God's disclosure in Christ. Consequently, the Black church and community have a theological mandate to engage in a Black sexual discourse of resistance whenever possible. Left now to determine is how precisely to respond to such a mandate.

CHAPTER 6

A Sexual Discourse of Resistance and the Black Church

What are the possibilities for a sexual discourse of resistance in the Black church? Can a church community move from regarding sexuality as a taboo issue to engaging in frank discussion about it? Is such a quantum change in attitudes possible? How is the Black church to address Black sexuality without alienating its members? Moreover, what are the implications of a sexual discourse of resistance for the church's activity? How can a sexual discourse of resistance be transforming? Appreciating that advocating and engaging in sexual discourse are easier said than done, this chapter offers creative suggestions on how Black churches can begin to provide an atmosphere conducive to engaging in a sexual discourse of resistance. After suggesting ways to foster a sexual discourse of resistance, this chapter will conclude by clarifying how the church is called to act in matters of sexuality.

REUNITING THE SACRED AND THE SECULAR

An essential first step toward a comprehensive treatment of Black sexuality by the Black church is to reestablish the unity of the sacred and secular realms. Many Black churches have already laid the groundwork for this by self-consciously attempting to affirm and reclaim their African heritage. In so doing, Black churches have integrated African symbols, rituals, chants, and dress into weekly worship. Yet this assertion and recovery of African roots typically ignores an essential part of African reality, the sacredness of secular reality. Despite the fact that the congregations are adorned in African regalia, drums are beaten, and African chants are recited, the ministers often preach on the evils of the worldly life of dance, sex, rap music, and so on. General denunciations

131

of secular reality, whether through damning exhortations or by making sure that it does not invade the church, belie the authenticity of an appreciation for one's African heritage. Derision of secular culture in Black churches defies the African religious roots of the Black faith tradition.

It cannot be said often enough that African worldviews tend not to make a distinction between sacred and secular realities. The very notion of secularity has no place in many African cultures. All that is of the world is of God. Every aspect of life presents an opportunity for the manifestation of the divine presence. According to many African traditions, there is a unity to life. Dualistic splits between the soul and body, heaven and earth, divine and flesh are nonexistent. No doubt because of their belief in the inherent unity between the sacred and secular, enslaved Africans were able to grasp the radicality of God's disclosure in Jesus. To be sure, this belief allowed Africans to celebrate sexuality as a sacred gift and opportunity.

Integral to reclaiming and affirming an African religious heritage, as well as to being conscientious stewards of the Black faith tradition, Black churches are obliged to restore the unity of the sacred and secular realms. Such restoration perhaps signals a fourth component to the meaning of wholeness for womanist theology. In her four-part definition of the womanist approach, Alice Walker certainly implies an appreciation for the oneness of the sacred and the secular when, in her list of loves, she says a womanist "Loves music. Loves dance. Loves the moon. *Loves* the spirit." Her nonhierarchical list of loves embraces things that stir the heart, the body, the mind, and the soul. Essentially, Walker's list suggests the inherent "wholeness" of reality that a womanist is bound to love. This means that in promoting wholeness for the Black community, womanist theologians are also constrained to spur the Black church toward an awareness of the inviolability of all reality, sacred and secular. Now, what does this have to do with nurturing a sexual discourse of resistance?

To view the sacred and secular as one dimension of living provides an atmosphere for reassessing the sanctity of human sexuality. It also suggests that what are traditionally considered secular resources may be used within the Black church to foster discourse on sexuality. Three "secular" resources, Black fictional literature and the music and movies of Black popular culture, can have an immediate impact in provoking discussion on Black sexuality.

BLACK LITERATURE: A CATALYST
FOR SEXUAL DISCOURSE

Historically, literature has been a "safe location" for many Black women to explore the unique experience of being Black and female in America. It is considered "safe" not in the sense of protecting these women from the consequences of what they may say, but in the sense that through fictional literature they have creatively and freely given voice to the "loves and troubles" of Black womanhood. Vital to their creative articulation of the vicissitudes of Black female living has been the exploration of the entanglements of Black sexuality. Sexuality is perhaps an inevitable theme of Black women's literature given the role played in the overall oppression of Black people by the exploitation of Black female sexuality, and given the centrality of Black women to the life struggle of Black families/communities. As has been previously demonstrated, the violation of Black women's sexuality has been the "gateway" to the corruption of Black sexuality in general. To impose upon the sexuality of Black women is to impose upon the way the entire community interacts.

Two novels in particular underscore the significance of Black women's sexuality to the life and wholeness of the Black community. First is Toni Morrison's award-winning novel *Beloved,* which tells the story of the impact of enslavement upon several generations of Black people. This story is told with an appreciation for an African awareness of time and sense of unity of life. The novel's structure is not linear, with no definite boundaries between past, present, and future. Rather, from the very beginning the reader is snatched into the middle of time and must be alert to the constant movement between past and present realities. Similarly, there are no boundaries between the living and the dead. Throughout a brilliantly woven story, Morrison tackles the taboo subject of Black reality that is yet the key to Black existence: Black sexuality.

The narrative revolves around a woman named Sethe, who chose to put her infant child, Beloved, to death in order to save her from experiencing the utterly inhumane tyranny of White racism, specifically enslavement. In the telling of her story, Sethe recalls being raped by several White, young men, an act that subsequently disrupted her whole life. From that moment on, Sethe's life was never the same. She viewed herself differently. Her relationship with her husband was virtually destroyed, and her relationship to her children became detached. Moreover, her experience of intimacy was distorted, and she became disconnected from her community. With the help of a visit from the ghost of Beloved, Sethe confronts her past, remembering as well as "disremembering." After coming face-to-face with her past, Sethe is soon able to find peace within herself and to reestablish life-enhancing relationships with the living and the dead.

In this thoughtfully complex story Morrison penetrates the co-nundrum of Black sexuality. She reveals how the White cultural manipulation of a Black woman's body, for the purposes of maintaining White patriarchal hegemony, frustrates an entire family's and commu-nity's wholeness because it corrupts the fullness of their sexuality. Only when one can boldly confront the past, and perhaps present, of White exploitation of Black sexuality can one achieve wholeness.

There is, perhaps, no better novel for penetrating Black sexual-ity than Alice Walker's much-discussed work (some have called it a womanist novel) *The Color Purple*. Through the letter writing of Celie, the main character, Walker ingeniously reveals how White hegemony has imposed upon the lives of Black people and set into motion a cycle of pathological and parasitic sexuality. Celie, a victim of sexual abuse at the hands of her father and husband (both of whom are acting out of a distorted sense of masculinity), has low self-esteem, a warped perspective on sex, dysfunctional relationships with women, and a sev-ered relationship with God. It is not until she develops a mutual and intimate (sexual but not simply genital) relationship with her female friend, Shug Avery, that Celie begins her journey toward wholeness. With Shug's guidance and counsel, Celie confronts her past, separat-ing fact from lie, and is subsequently and painstakingly restored to a healthy sexuality. In being able to celebrate her sexuality, Celie redis-covers herself, reconnects with her sister, reestablishes community, and re-envisions God. Indeed, one of the culminating moments in Celie's quest for wholeness is her movement toward rejecting a God that looks like a White man and accepting a God that loves and is indeed inside of her own Black, female, embodied self. Shug exhorts Celie:

> Here's the thing, say Shug. The thing I believe. God is inside you and inside everybody else. You come into the world with God. But only them that search for it inside find it. And sometimes it just manifest itself even if you not looking, or don't know what you looking for.[1]

In this moment of Shug's prodding Celie to find the God that is inside of her, Walker succinctly captures the comprehensive nature of human sexuality — it is that which puts one in "right" relationship to oneself, hence to others, and ultimately to God.

Given the depth of White sexual exploitation of Black lives, it is not surprising that numerous other novels tell the story of Black people's experience by creatively unraveling the sexual politics of the Black community. Audre Lorde does this through her biomythography *Zami,* in which she passionately relates her growing up in Harlem and her self-discovery of her lesbian sexuality. She provides an intimate insight into a mother-daughter relationship, the racism found in gay and lesbian communities, and the heterosexism and sexism of the Black community. Similarly, there is no Black male writer who provides a more poignant commentary on being Black, male, and gay than James Baldwin in his many novels. Contemporary Black, gay novelist E. Lynn Harris also provides compelling portraits of the complex reality of being Black and gay in America.

In an effort to establish a nonintimidating environment for engaging in sexual discourse, Black churches might institute regular book discussion groups. Through discussions of selective Black novels such as *Beloved* or *The Color Purple,* Black churchpeople would be impelled toward undertaking sexual discourse. A discussion of the realities of Black sexuality, including male/female relationships, self-esteem, and sexual intimacy, would be almost unavoidable. Most significantly, these novels would assist persons in recognizing the interconnections between Black sexuality and White racism, as well as how distortions of Black sexuality have impacted Black intimacy and relationships. Such a program of regular study would not only advance critical sexual discourse but also foster literacy in terms of Black literature.

BLACK SEXUALITY AND POPULAR CULTURE

In addition to engaging Black literature, an appreciation for the sanctity of secular reality would also allow the Black church to get in touch with Black hip-hop culture. Just as literature has engaged Black sexuality, so too has Black popular culture, even if it has most often done so in a manner contrary to Black life and wholeness.

For instance, as noted earlier, many have recognized the obsession with sex that seems to be a part of the hip-hop culture of Black youth. Movies, songs, and gangsta rap are replete with tales of sexual promiscuity, misogynism, gay-bashing, and perverted views of masculinity. We cannot avoid noting that the popular culture of Black youth reveals a side of Black sexuality. Typically, popular culture also offers a portrait of Black spirituality as movies or song lyrics variously speak of God. It is imperative, therefore, that Black churches not dismiss hip-hop. The music, movies, and literature of this culture are an entree for discussing Black sexuality. Various elements of this culture can be valuable tools for examining the messages about sex, intimate relationships, and masculinity and femininity that Black youth receive, as well as for exploring the impetus behind the messages. To advance such discussion, Black churches might institute a movie/music night for viewing and discussing certain popular films or music videos. Again, this could be a beginning for more fully exploring the concerns that surround teenage sexuality.

BIBLE STUDY

Finally, to appreciate what is traditionally considered secular is not to ignore the sacred. None of these proposed activities (book study, movie/music nights) should take the place of what is typically the center of any Black church program — Bible study. But again, Bible study must be approached in such a way that a creative engagement in sexual discourse can occur. This means that Bible study should provide an opportunity for personal inspiration *and* serious reflection on complex issues, such as sexuality. To achieve this, the work of Black biblical scholars should become integral to church Bible studies. As suggested in previous chapters, Black biblical scholars are too often unappreciated in many Black churches. Yet many of these scholars have painstakingly tried to explore biblical texts in light of the Black experience and in a manner that is respectful and affirming of the Black biblical tradition. Their expertise must be utilized by the Black church community.

In addition, as preaching has been the centerpiece of the Black church tradition, teaching must also become central. This means that as churches regularly spend thousands of dollars to engage the services of the country's top preachers, they too must be willing to spend money to engage Black scholars and theologians. If a church's budget clarifies that church's priorities, then it goes without saying that theological education is a low priority in far too many Black churches. A theological education week must become as essential to Black church programming as are spring revival weeks. Too often, Black churches are willing to spend money for preachers, but not for scholars. They must be committed to pay for both. If indeed Black churchpeople are going to fully appreciate their rich religious heritage and its uniqueness and to critique it and grow in relation to it, then they will have to engage in theological scholarship. In fact, Black and womanist theologians cannot carry out their prophetic work if they do not have access to Black churches. Just as Black religious scholars are accountable to their Black church communities, so must Black churches be responsible to these Black scholars. This means that Black church leadership must institutionalize regular dialogue between the Black church and the Black academy. Again, such dialogue will be invaluable in fostering possibilities for exploring Black sexuality.

FROM PEW TO PULPIT

As significant as the programs suggested above may be to creating an atmosphere within the church conducive to engaging in a sexual discourse of resistance, there is something even more fundamental to be considered. In Michel Foucault's discussion of power and resistance, he suggests that if the way people relate on the microlevels of society are changed, then perhaps the way power is institutionalized will also change. This observation is very instructive for our discussion of how to nurture a Black sexual discourse within Black church communities. The change in attitude toward sexuality within the Black church and wider community must begin not at the top with Black church leadership or theologians, but at the bottom with the people who sit in the pews. Most particularly, a new Black perspective on sexuality must begin with those who constitute over 70 percent of Black church congregations, Black women.

If Black women have indeed been the gateway to White culture's exploitation of Black sexuality, they may also be the key to reclaiming Black sexuality. As has been shown in Toni Morrison's *Beloved* and Alice Walker's *The Color Purple*, when Black women are able to affirm themselves and come to a healthy sense of their own sexuality, patterns of relationships are transformed for the entire Black community. The task of womanist theology is therefore clear. To be a *womanist* theologian is to enable Black women to "love themselves, regardless." As womanist theologians we must be ever resolute in our task of empowering the Black women who sit in the pews to be able fervently to affirm and love every aspect of their embodied selves. To do so, womanist theology is obliged to reconnect Black women to their history and rich heritage as Black women. Black women's fiction, biographies, testimonies, diaries, and various writings that relate Black women's

experiences must remain a core source of womanist theological reflection. These stories must be told. They are crucial to empowering other
Black women. They are integral to helping Black women connect to
themselves.

There has been no greater moment for me in teaching a course on
womanist theology than when numerous Black women exclaim at the
end of the course a new confidence in themselves as they have been
connected to their own rich experience as Black women. And this hap-
pens year after year. As one woman told me, "I discovered in this course
that there was nothing wrong with me; it was simply the experience
of being Black and female." What does Black women's reconciliation
to themselves mean for the life and wholeness of the entire Black
community and for the possibility of a sexual discourse of resistance?

First, self-love is crucial to a healthy attitude toward one's own sexuality. As mentioned earlier, to love oneself is to be able to love others as
well as God. Second, if Black women are to be able to affirm the fullness
of their sexuality, then they must claim that power within themselves
that urges them toward life and wholeness. It is that "passion" within
that compels them to resist anything that would frustrate Black life
and wholeness at the same time that it propels them into creative, life-
affirming activity. For Black women to be able to affirm themselves is for
them to be in touch with that "most profoundly creative source, . . . that
which is female and self-affirming in the face of a racist, patriarchal,
and anti-erotic society."[2]

If Black women are empowered toward self-love and hence are able
to affirm their sexuality — their "passion" for life — then the call for a
sexual discourse of resistance would seem inevitable. For Black women
to be in touch with their very passion means that they would not succor
anything that would deny their life and humanity or the life and humanity of others. Such passion would compel them toward the kind of
sexual discourse that would expose the life-threatening sexual politics of
the Black community that impairs relationships and denies full humanity to persons because of their gender or sexual orientation. Given Black
women's significant presence within Black churches, if they demanded
discourse relating to matters of Black sexuality, Black churches would
have to consent, in order to survive. Without a doubt, when Black
women are empowered and enabled to affirm the fullness of their humanity, the entire Black community will be closer to keeping faith with
God's radical disclosure in Jesus. This brings us to the major challenge
of a sexual discourse of resistance.

SEXUAL DISCOURSE: A CALL TO ACTION

If a discourse is truly disruptive, it not only transforms the way people think, but also significantly affects the way they act. In fact, disruptive words without disruptive action become only a camouflage for continuing life-negating and oppressive practices. It's a cliché, but actions do speak far louder than words. Promoting an awareness and understanding of the complex history that has shaped Black people's responses to sexual issues is only one aspect of a sexual discourse of resistance. A second major concern is to get the Black church to act a different way in regard to sexual issues. While White culture might bear the burden for manipulating Black sexuality and even Black people's responses to their own sexuality, Black people are, in the end, responsible for their actions. A sexual discourse of resistance signals that it is time for a change. It demands a transformation in the way the Black church community, especially its leaders, has conducted itself in terms of women and gay and lesbian persons.

For far too long the Black church has gotten away with behaviors that simply malign and pervert the humanity of others. It has too often frustrated the expression of a healthy, life-enhancing sexuality for many members of the Black community. For example, the homophobia of the Black church is often as venomous as that expressed in some gangsta rap. More disturbing, however, is that the Black church has the power to impose its homophobic beliefs upon others, thus affecting the way people live their lives. And, to be sure, homophobia has been the basis for the Black church's negligent response to the HIV/AIDS crisis.

A sexual discourse of resistance makes clear that there is no longer an excuse for the Black church behaving in such a way that compromises the humanity or mocks the sexuality of any individual. It is time for a transformation. Such a transformation begins with the Black church community becoming loud advocates for those who are marginalized, outcast, or oppressed in society because of who they are. The ministry of Jesus, the incarnate one, clarifies that sinners are those who foster racism, sexism, and homophobia and those who nurture racist, sexist, and heterosexist structures and systems. For the church to be homophobic and heterosexist is for the church to be Antichrist.

James Cone once said that whiteness as it symbolized racism was of the Antichrist. Cone was right, because that which would distort, malign, or interfere with the humanity of another is the very antithesis of who Jesus was as the perfect revelation of God. Such is the case with homophobia. This is the very antithesis of God's disclosure in Jesus.

This also means that we who call ourselves Christians are constrained to denounce and to tear down those interlocking structures and systems of racist, sexist, and classist oppression that grant privilege to those who may be the right color, right gender, and express their sexuality in an acceptable way. The radicality of God's disclosure in Jesus means that we are called not to try to garner privilege in this interlocking system, but to eradicate such an unjust system of privilege. And, to be sure, the Black church is not to duplicate such an interlocking system of oppression by establishing its own hierarchy of privilege and power. To date, it has done just this in its attempts to exclude women and gay and lesbian persons from the places of power within the institution.

To go one step further, the church's advocacy for the rights of others implies the church's consistent involvement in the struggle against HIV/AIDS. The Black church cannot continue to ignore what has been and is so devastating to Black life and well-being. It is no longer acceptable to hide behind fears of the disease. If such fears exist, they can be quickly alleviated by the Black church availing itself of medical expertise to clarify the manner in which the disease is transmitted. Fears notwithstanding, it is no doubt the Black church's attitude toward homosexuality that has hindered its response. A sexual discourse of resistance, in highlighting the sin of homophobia, stresses that sin is any activity that frustrates Black life. The Black church's negligence in regard to HIV/AIDS is nothing less than sin because such negligence frustrates Black life. Black churches have no choice but to initiate and participate in HIV/AIDS ministries.

No longer must pastors be seen as having the answers to all the Black community's concerns. Individual pastors cannot be the center of all the church's activity. Black churches must engage in shared ministries. Pastors must enlist the help not only of other pastors, but of laity who have certain expertise in dealing with particular concerns.

The Black church must move toward a ministry that is more responsive to the complex issues of Black living. Such a ministry is not based upon the charismatic personality of one individual. Instead, it empowers the community it serves to actively participate, sharing their skills, in a ministry of life and wholeness for Black men and women.

Finally, if the Black church community really believes in the justice of God and the inherent worth of all individuals, then this community must hold its leaders accountable for their misconduct. If Black men and women are ever to come to a healthy appreciation of their own sexuality, then Black church leaders must not be permitted to mock the sexuality of others. In this regard, though beyond the particular scope of this book, it will be important to explore how Black attitudes toward sexuality have impacted the response of Black churches to domestic violence and sexual misconduct among clergy. A sexual discourse of resistance makes clear in no uncertain terms that enough is enough, that it is time for the Black church to change not only its attitudes toward sexuality but also its behavior.

THE NATIONAL RELIGIOUS SUMMIT ON BLACK SEXUALITY

That the Black religious community in general is beginning to recognize the urgent need for a sexual discourse of resistance and a change in Black church conduct was made clear with the calling of the First National Black Religious Summit on Sexuality. This conference was held June 12 and 13, 1997, at the Howard University School of Divinity in Washington, D.C. It was organized by the Reverend Carlton Veazey under the auspices of the Religious Coalition for Reproductive Choice. Entitled "Breaking the Silence," this conference represented a monumental stride toward engaging the Black religious community in a sustained sexual discourse of resistance geared toward changing the way the church and its leaders act in regard to sexual issues.

The conference organizers attempted to address the full spectrum of Black sexuality. Informative and provocative workshops were held on teenage pregnancy, domestic violence, HIV/AIDS, male responsibility, sexuality education for the Black church, and substance abuse. The breadth of the workshops signified the recognition of the comprehensive nature of human sexuality, even though the relationship between sexuality and spirituality was not emphasized, as evidenced by the lack of Bible study. Moreover, the conference failed to engage serious issues of sexism and homophobia in the Black church and community, as it did not address the interrelationship between the exploitation of Black sexuality and racist, sexist, classist, and heterosexist structures of oppression.

However, limitations notwithstanding, the fact that the conference took place conceivably signals a new readiness in terms of Black church conversation. Given that hundreds of Black churchpeople from across the country were willing to gather at a two-day conference on Black sexuality, perhaps the time has come for Black religious and certainly theological leadership to say a new thing about sexuality and God and for Black people to act in a new way.[3] To be sure, maintaining the silence on issues of Black sexuality is exacting too high a price from the Black community.

CONCLUDING CHALLENGE

There is a life-defying brokenness in the Black community. Black women and men, girls and boys, are losing the battle for self-love. Intimate relationships between men and women are dangerously strained. The community is ravaged by teenage pregnancies, homicide, HIV/AIDS, domestic violence, and even sexual misconduct among clergy and other Black leaders. Moreover, the Black church, which has traditionally been a sanctuary of life and freedom for Black people, has been shamefully unresponsive to these issues even while it provides a sacred canopy for sexist and heterosexist structures and behavior. Indeed, the conditions are right for Black genocide if something does not happen to break the hold that White culture has had over Black people's bodies, psyches, and spiritualities. A modern and transformative discourse must begin.

The hope for Black life and Black wholeness is inextricably linked to the strident initiation of a Black sexual discourse of resistance that disrupts the Black church's and community's very way of being. The Black community needs this discourse to help it to understand the role of Black sexuality in maintaining the White hegemonic, racist, sexist, classist, and heterosexist structures. A sexual discourse of resistance is needed also to help Black men and women recognize how the White cultural exploitation of Black sexuality has corrupted Black people's concepts of themselves, one another, and their God. Finally, it is needed to chart a new way of acting in regard to sexual concerns. It is the necessary first step toward living out the radicality of God's disclosure in Jesus.

Black churchmen and churchwomen often confess in song, "I've decided to make Jesus my choice." The time has come for Black church-people to understand the profound meaning of this choice in relation to who they are as sexual beings. To choose Jesus as the center of one's life and faith is to choose one whose very being and way of be-ing in the world compel an appreciation for the sanctity of human sexuality. Thus, to render sexuality a taboo issue is, in effect, to preclude the possibility of knowing the full measure of God's intimate presence and activity in human history. It is virtually to close oneself off from the very God who hears, knows, and walks with Black people in their struggles for life and wholeness. Only when the veil of silence surrounding Black sexuality is lifted will Black men and women be able to realize the liberating significance of what it means for the God of Jesus Christ to have chosen them.

Finally, the Great Commandment makes the need for redeeming the sacredness of sexuality clear. It resolves, "You shall love the Lord your God with all your heart, all your soul, and all your mind. You shall love your neighbor as yourself." Such a resolution is a call to radical wholeness. It summons women and men to wholly love their spiritual and embodied selves so that they can wholly love their God. Only when the taboo of sexuality is discarded will Black women and men be free to experience what it means to wholly love and be loved by the God that became flesh in Jesus.

Notes

Introduction

1. Renee Hill, "Who Are We for Each Other? Sexism, Sexuality, and Womanist Theology," in *Black Theology: A Documentary History, 1980–1992*, vol. 2, ed. James Cone and Gayraud Wilmore (Maryknoll, N.Y.: Orbis Books, 1993), 345–46.

2. It should be noted that ethicist Cheryl Sanders did not ignore the aspect of Walker's definition that affirms gay/lesbian ways of being. Sanders indeed argued against the appropriateness of adopting womanist nomenclature for Christian theological discourse because of its approval of same-sexed relationships. See Cheryl Sanders, "Christian Ethics and Theology in Womanist Perspective," *Journal of Feminist Studies in Religion* 5, no. 2 (fall 1989).

3. Quoted in Sheryl Gay Stolberg, "Eyes Shut, Black America Is Being Ravaged by AIDS," *New York Times,* June 29, 1998.

4. Ibid.

5. Toinette Eugene, "How Can We Forget? An Ethic of Care for AIDS, the African American Family, and the Black Catholic Church," in *Embracing the Spirit: Womanist Perspectives on Hope, Salvation, and Transformation,* ed. Emilie M. Townes (Maryknoll, N.Y.: Orbis Books, 1998), 271.

6. Emilie M. Townes, *In a Blaze of Glory: Womanist Spirituality as Social Witness* (Nashville: Abingdon Press, 1995). See especially chapter 4, "Writing the Right: Gender and Sexuality in the African American Community," 68–88.

7. Karen Baker-Fletcher and Garth Kasimu Baker-Fletcher, *My Sister, My Brother: Womanist and Xodus God-Talk* (Maryknoll, N.Y.: Orbis Books, 1997), 259.

8. James B. Nelson, *Embodiment: An Approach to Sexuality and Christian Theology* (Minneapolis: Augsburg Publishing House, 1978), 17–18.

1: Black Sexuality: A Pawn of White Culture

1. These hearings were held in October 1991. Three days were spent focused solely on the Hill sexual harassment accusation. For a complete transcript, see Anita Miller, ed., *The Complete Transcripts of the Clarence Thomas–Anita Hill Hearings: October 11, 12, 13, 1991* (Chicago: Academy Chicago Publishers, 1994).

2. bell hooks, *Black Looks: Race and Representation* (Boston: South End Press, 1992), 85.

3. More will be said about both the Thomas hearings and the Simpson trial in chapter 2 in relation to Black sexual stereotypes.

4. hooks, *Black Looks*, 84.

5. James Baldwin, *The Price of the Ticket* (New York: St. Martin's/Marek, 1985), xix–xx.

6. Cornel West, *Prophesy Deliverance: An Afro-American Revolutionary Christianity* (Philadelphia: Westminster Press, 1982). See chapter 2, "The Genealogy of Modern Racism."

7. Ibid., 54.

8. Winthrop Jordan, *White over Black: American Attitudes toward the Negro, 1550–1812* (Chapel Hill: University of North Carolina Press, 1968), 242.

9. Ibid., 248.

10. For more on this see George M. Fredrickson, *The Black Image in the White Mind: The Debate on Afro-American Character and Destiny, 1817–1914* (Middleton, Conn.: Wesleyan University Press, 1987). See especially chapter 3, "Science, Polygenesis, and the Proslavery Argument."

11. Quoted in Jordan, *White over Black*, 248.

12. Ibid., 248–49.

13. Ibid., 518ff.

14. Quoted in ibid., 515.

15. Quoted in ibid., 258.

16. Quoted in Fredrickson, *Black Image*, 47.

17. Manning Marable, "Blacks Should Emphasize Their Ethnicity," in *Racism in America: Opposing Viewpoints*, ed. William Dudley and Charles Cozic (San Diego: Greenhaven Press, 1991), 180.

18. Ibid.

19. See the definition of culture in the *Dictionary of Feminist Theologies* (Louisville: Westminster/John Knox Press, 1996), 63.

20. Baldwin, *Price of the Ticket*, xix–xx.

21. See Audre Lorde, *Sister Outsider* (Freedom, Calif.: The Crossing Press, 1984), esp. 110ff.

22. Jeffrey Weeks, *Sex, Politics, and Society: The Regulation of Sexuality since 1800* (New York: Longman Group, 1981), 7.

23. Jana Sawicki, *Disciplining Foucault: Feminism, Power, and the Body* (New York: Routledge, 1991), 23.

24. Michel Foucault, *The History of Sexuality: An Introduction*, vol. 1, trans. Robert Hurley (New York: Vintage Books, 1990), 95–96.

25. Sawicki, *Disciplining Foucault*, 23.

26. Foucault, *History of Sexuality*, 101. It should also be noted that Foucault recognizes the subversive nature of discourse. He says that it can also be utilized to resist power. We will discuss this further in a later chapter.

27. Quoted in James Miller, *The Passion of Michel Foucault* (New York: Doubleday/Anchor Books, 1993), 293.

28. Foucault, *History of Sexuality,* 107.

29. Cornel West, *Race Matters* (Boston: Beacon Press, 1993), 85.

30. Patricia Hill Collins, *Black Feminist Thought: Knowledge, Consciousness, and the Politics of Empowerment* (Boston: Unwin Hyman, 1990), 165.

31. John D'Emilio and Estelle B. Freedman, *Intimate Matters: A History of Sexuality in America* (New York: Harper and Row, 1988), 86.

32. See William C. Placher, *A History of Christian Theology: An Introduction* (Philadelphia: Westminster Press, 1983), 108.

33. See St. Augustine, *The City of God,* bk. 14, chap. 16.

34. Carter Heyward, "Notes on Historical Grounding: Beyond Sexual Essentialism," in *Sexuality and the Sacred: Sources for Theological Reflection,* ed. James B. Nelson and Sandra P. Longfellow (Louisville: Westminster/John Knox Press, 1994), 12.

35. Michel Foucault, "Sexuality and Solitude," in *Michel Foucault: Ethics Subjectivity and Truth: The Essential Works of Foucault, 1954–1984,* vol. 1, ed. Paul Rabinow (New York: New Press, 1997), 180.

36. Ibid., 180.

37. These dualistic philosophies are given this label by James B. Nelson in *Embodiment: An Approach to Sexuality and Christian Theology* (Minneapolis: Augsburg Publishing House, 1978), 46.

38. Renita Weems, *Battered Love: Marriage, Sex, and Violence in the Hebrew Prophets* (Minneapolis: Fortress Press, 1995), 5.

39. Quoted in Nelson, *Embodiment,* 60.

40. John J. McNeil, *The Church and the Homosexual,* 3d ed. (Boston: Beacon Press, 1988), 94.

41. Nelson, *Embodiment,* 46.

42. Rosemary Ruether, *New Woman, New Earth: Sexist Ideologies and Human Liberation* (New York: Seabury, 1975), 3–4.

2: Stereotypes, False Images, Terrorism: The White Assault upon Black Sexuality

1. Patricia Hill Collins, *Black Feminist Thought: Knowledge, Consciousness, and the Politics of Empowerment* (Boston: Unwin Hyman, 1990), 68.

2. Winthrop Jordan, *White over Black: American Attitudes toward the Negro, 1550–1812* (Chapel Hill: University of North Carolina Press, 1968), 4.

3. Quoted in ibid., 4.

4. Quoted in ibid., 33.

5. Quoted in ibid., 30.

6. Quoted in ibid., 31.

7. Ibid., 32.

8. See Sander L. Gilman, "Black Bodies, White Bodies: Toward an Iconography of Female Sexuality in Late Nineteenth-Century Art, Medicine, and

Literature," in *Race, Writing, and Difference*, ed. Henry Lewis Gates Jr. (Chicago: University of Chicago Press, 1987), 231.

9. Ibid., 235.

10. Ibid., 235.

11. Gilman and others have noted that Bartmann's sexual parts remained on display into the twenty-first century. I have not been able to confirm whether or not they still are on exhibit in Paris.

12. Deborah Gray White, *Ar'n't I a Woman? Female Slaves in the Ante-bellum South* (New York: Norton, 1985), 27–28.

13. Collins, *Black Feminist Thought*, 164.

14. Robert Staples, *The Black Woman in America: Sex, Marriage, and the Family* (Chicago: Nelson-Hall Publishers, 1973), 37.

15. White, *Ar'n't I a Woman?* 29.

16. Jordan, *White over Black*, 35.

17. See interview of Tabb Gross and Lewis Smith in John Blassingame, ed., *Slave Testimony: Two Centuries of Letters, Speeches, Interviews, and Autobiographies* (Baton Rouge: Louisiana State University Press, 1977), 347.

18. Ibid., 502.

19. See James Mellon, ed., *Bullwhip Days: The Slaves Remember, an Oral History* (New York: Avon Books, 1988), 292.

20. Ibid., 147.

21. Ibid., 287.

22. White, *Ar'n't I a Woman?* 31.

23. Ibid., 29.

24. See Leon Litwack, *Trouble in Mind: Black Southerners in the Age of Jim Crow* (New York: Alfred A. Knopf, 1998), 349.

25. Ibid., 344.

26. See Blassingame, *Slave Testimony*, 221.

27. Ibid., 157.

28. White, *Ar'n't I a Woman?* 61.

29. Patricia Morton, *Disfigured Images: The Historical Assault on Afro-American Women* (Westport, Conn.: Praeger, 1991), 10.

30. White, *Ar'n't I a Woman?* 61.

31. Blassingame, *Slave Testimony*, 132–33.

32. Catherine Clinton, *The Plantation Mistress: Woman's World in the Old South* (New York: Pantheon/Random House, 1982), 201–2.

33. Quoted in Collins, *Black Feminist Thought*, 72.

34. Ibid.

35. White, *Ar'n't I a Woman?* 58, 61.

36. Quoted in Paula Giddings, "The Last Taboo," in *Race-ing Justice, En-gendering Power*, ed. Toni Morrison (New York: Pantheon, 1992), 444.

37. Jordan, *White over Black*, 158.

38. Richard Wright, "Black Boy (American Hunger)," in *Richard Wright:*

Later Works, ed. Arnold Rampersad (New York: Library of America Edition, 1981), 180.

39. Giddings, "Last Taboo," 451.

40. Quoted in Herbert Gutman, *The Black Family in Slavery and Freedom: 1750–1925* (New York: Vintage Books, 1976), 388.

41. Manning Marable, "The Black Male: Searching beyond Stereotypes," in *The American Black Male: His Present Status and His Future,* ed. Richard G. Majors and Jacob U. Gordon (Chicago: Nelson-Hall Publishers, 1994), 71.

42. Litwack, *Trouble in Mind,* 344.

43. Jordan, *White over Black,* 156.

44. Litwack, *Trouble in Mind,* 302.

45. Gutman, *Black Family,* 390.

46. White, *Ar'n't I a Woman?* 164–65.

47. Gutman, *Black Family,* 389.

48. Ida B. Wells, *On Lynchings: Southern Horrors* (New York: Arno, 1969 [1892]), 6.

49. Litwack, *Trouble in Mind,* 307.

50. Hazel Carby, "'On the Threshold of Women's Era': Lynching, Empire, and Sexuality in Black Feminist Theory," in *Race, Writing, and Difference,* 308.

51. White, *Ar'n't I a Woman?* 165.

52. Patricia Hill Collins, "The Meaning of Motherhood in Black Culture and Black Mother-Daughter Relationships," in *Double Stitch: Black Women Write about Mothers and Daughters,* ed. Patricia Bell-Scott et al. (New York: HarperPerennial, 1991), 44.

53. "The Moynihan Report: The Negro Family: The Case for National Action," in *Black Matriarchy: Myth or Reality?* ed. John H. Bracey Jr., August Meier, and Elliott Rudwick (Belmont, Calif.: Wadsworth, 1971).

54. Paul Gilroy, "It's a Family Affair," in *Black Popular Culture* (a project by Michelle Wallace), ed. Gina Dent (Seattle: Bay Press, 1992), 312.

55. Ibid.

56. Collins, *Black Feminist Thought,* 75.

57. Ibid., 78.

58. Audre Lorde, "Scratching the Surface: Some Notes on Barriers to Women and Loving," in *Sister Outsider* (Freedom, Calif.: The Crossing Press, 1984), 45.

59. Collins, *Black Feminist Thought,* 77.

60. Ibid., 78.

61. This story is recounted in numerous sources. See, for instance, Christine Stansell, "White Feminist and Black Realities," in *Race-ing Justice, En-gendering Power,* 260–61.

62. Nell Painter, "Hill, Thomas, and the Use of Racial Stereotype," in *Race-ing Justice, En-gendering Power,* 209.

63. Anita Miller, ed., *The Complete Transcripts of the Clarence Thomas–Anita*

Hill Hearings: October 11, 12, 13, 1991 (Chicago: Academy Chicago Publishers, 1994), 142–43.

64. Ibid., 152.

65. Ibid., 139–40.

66. Ibid., 157.

67. See, for instance, the testimony of John Dogget in *The Complete Transcripts*, 367–72.

68. Anita Hill, *Speaking Truth to Power* (New York: Doubleday, 1997), 196.

69. Painter, "Hill, Thomas, and the Use of Racial Stereotype," 212–13.

70. Ishmael Reed, "Bigger and O. J.," in *Birth of a Nation'hood: Gaze, Script, and Spectacle in the O. J. Simpson Case*, ed. Toni Morrison and Claudia Brodsky Lacour (New York: Pantheon, 1997), 170–71.

71. Kimberle Williams Crenshaw, "Color-blind Dreams and Racial Nightmares: Reconfiguring Racism in the Post–Civil Rights Era," in *Birth of a Nation'hood*, 113.

72. Toni Morrison, introduction to *Birth of a Nation'hood*, xxvii–xxviii.

3: The Legacy of White Sexual Assault

1. Patricia Hill Collins identifies a culture of resistance as a part of Black women's struggle in particular. She says this culture "contains contradictory elements that foster both compliance with and resistance to oppression." See *Black Feminist Thought: Knowledge, Consciousness, and the Politics of Empowerment* (Boston: Unwin Hyman, 1990), 18n4. Borrowing from Hill Collins I use "culture of resistance" to point to the various ways in which Black people resisted their oppression, be it through song, prayer, nurturing communal and family networks, or more active means of rebellion.

2. Herbert Gutman, *The Black Family in Slavery and Freedom: 1750–1925* (New York: Vintage Books, 1976), 61.

3. John D'Emilio and Estelle B. Freedman, *Intimate Matters: A History of Sexuality in America* (New York: Harper and Row, 1988), 187.

4. John Blassingame, *The Slave Community: Plantation Life in the Ante-bellum South* (New York: Oxford University Press, 1979), 162. It should be noted, however, that this concept of defloration and, in some instances, female castration, while still put into practice in some African societies, is not without criticism for its brutality as well as the sexist ideology that often accompanies it.

5. See ibid., 164–65.

6. Robert Staples, *Introduction to Black Sociology* (New York: McGraw-Hill Book Company, 1976), 119.

7. Quoted in Blassingame, *Slave Community*, 171.

8. Gutman, *Black Family*, 71.

9. Quoted in ibid., 71.

10. Cornel West, *Race Matters* (Boston: Beacon Press, 1993), 86.

11. See Paula Giddings, "The Last Taboo," in *Race-ing Justice, En-gendering Power*, ed. Toni Morrison (New York: Pantheon, 1992), 442.

12. See Emilie M. Townes, *In a Blaze of Glory: Womanist Spirituality as Social Witness* (Nashville: Abingdon Press, 1995), chap. 4, "Writing the Right."

13. Comment made at a lecture I gave to the New York chapter of the Union of Black Episcopalians in spring 1997.

14. West, *Race Matters*, 86.

15. Giddings, "Last Taboo," 442.

16. Michel Foucault, *The History of Sexuality: An Introduction*, vol. 1, trans. Robert Hurley (New York: Vintage Books, 1990), 101.

17. Ibid., 101.

18. Angela Davis, *Blues Legacies and Black Feminism: Gertrude "Ma" Rainey, Bessie Smith, and Billie Holiday* (New York: Pantheon, 1998), 5.

19. Ibid., 4.

20. Ibid., 46.

21. Ibid., 107.

22. Ibid., 53.

23. Michael Dyson, *Between God and Gangsta Rap: Bearing Witness to Black Culture* (New York: Oxford University Press, 1996), 177.

24. For more concerning marketplace morality, see West, *Race Matters*, 17ff.

25. Dyson, *Between God and Gangsta Rap*, 178.

26. Ibid.

27. This designation of Black literature as a safe location is taken from Patricia Hill Collins, who argues that literature has provided one of the "safe spaces" for Black women, in particular, to conduct independent explorations of their experiences. See Collins, *Black Feminist Thought*.

28. Cheryl Townsend Gilkes, "The Womanist Challenge to Cultural Humiliation and Community Ambivalence," in *A Troubling in My Soul: Womanist Perspectives on Evil and Suffering*, ed. Emilie M. Townes (Maryknoll, N.Y.: Orbis Books, 1993), 245.

29. Toinette Eugene, "While Love Is Unfashionable: Ethical Implications of Black Spirituality and Sexuality," in *Sexuality and the Sacred: Sources for Theological Reflection*, ed. James B. Nelson and Sandra P. Longfellow (Louisville: Westminster/John Knox Press, 1994), 108–9.

30. Recounted with the permission of Yvette Abrahams, a South African scholar, as she told this story during a womanist dialogue on the Internet.

31. See Leon Dash, *When Children Want Children: The Urban Crisis of Teenage Childbearing* (New York: William Morrow and Company, 1989), 11.

32. Ibid., 30.

33. West, *Race Matters*, 85.

34. Toni Morrison, *Beloved* (New York: Albert A. Knopf, 1988), 88–89.

35. bell hooks, "'Whose Pussy Is This?' A Feminist Comment," in *Talking Back: Thinking Feminist, Thinking Black* (Boston: South End Press, 1989), 137.

36. bell hooks, *Black Looks: Race and Representation* (Boston: South End Press, 1992), 63–64.

37. Ibid., 105–6.

38. Michael Dyson, *Race Rules* (Boston: Addison-Wesley, 1996), 203.

39. Ibid., 201.

40. bell hooks and Cornel West, *Breaking Bread: Insurgent Black Intellectual Life* (Boston: South End Press, 1991), 115.

41. hooks, *Black Looks*, 89.

42. Collins, *Black Feminist Thought*, 185–86.

43. hooks, *Black Looks*, 98.

44. Quoted in James H. Cone and Gayraud Wilmore, eds., *Black Theology: A Documentary History, 1966–1979*, vol. 1 (Maryknoll, N.Y.: Orbis Books, 1993), 37–39.

45. Eugene, "While Love Is Unfashionable," 106.

46. Peter Paris, *The Spirituality of African Peoples: The Search for a Common Moral Discourse* (Minneapolis: Fortress Press, 1995), 27.

4: Homophobia and Heterosexism in the Black Church and Community

1. Angela Davis, *Blues Legacies and Black Feminism* (New York: Pantheon, 1998), 131.

2. See, for instance, Robin Scroggs, *The New Testament and Homosexuality* (Philadelphia: Fortress Press, 1983); John McNeil, *The Church and the Homosexual* (Kansas City: Sheed, Andrews and McMeel, 1976); L. D. Scanzoni and V. R. Mollencott, *Is the Homosexual My Neighbor? A Positive Christian Response*, rev. ed. (San Francisco: Harper and Row, 1994).

3. John Boswell, *Christianity, Social Tolerance, and Homosexuality* (Chicago: University of Chicago Press, 1980), 117.

4. Vincent Wimbush, "The Bible and African Americans: An Outline of an Interpretative History," in *Stony the Road We Trod: African American Biblical Interpretation*, ed. Cain Hope Felder (Minneapolis: Fortress Press, 1991), 82.

5. Ibid., 83.

6. Renita Weems, "Reading Her Way through the Struggle: African American Women and the Bible," in *Stony the Road We Trod*, 57–58.

7. Wimbush, "The Bible and African Americans," 85.

8. Ibid., 85.

9. Weems, "Reading Her Way," 61.

10. Ibid., 70.

11. Wimbush, "The Bible and African Americans," 84.

12. Ibid., 86.

13. Weems, "Reading Her Way," 60–61.

14. Wimbush, "The Bible and African Americans," 88.

15. William H. Myers, "The Hermeneutical Dilemma of the African American Biblical Student," in *Stony the Road We Trod*, 41.

16. Ibid.

17. Barbara Smith and Beverly Smith, "Across the Kitchen Table: A Sister to Sister Dialogue," in *This Bridge Called My Back: Writing by Radical Women of Color*, ed. Cherríe Moraga and Gloria Anzaldúa (New York: Kitchen Table/ Women of Color Press, 1983), 124.

18. Frances Cress Welsing, *The Isis Papers: The Keys to the Colors* (Chicago: Third World Press, 1991), 81.

19. Molefi Kete Asante, *Afrocentricity* (Trenton, N.J.: African World Press, 1988), 57.

20. Keith Boykin, *One More River to Cross: Black and Gay in America* (New York: Anchor Books/Doubleday, 1996), 194. See also Colin Spencer, *Homosexuality in History* (New York: Harcourt Brace and Company, 1995).

21. Audre Lorde, "Scratching the Surface: Some Notes on Barriers to Women and Loving," in *Sister Outsider* (Freedom, Calif.: The Crossing Press, 1984), 49–50.

22. Smith and Smith, "Across the Kitchen Table," 125.

23. Rhonda Williams, "Living at the Crossroads: Explorations in Race, Nationality, Sexuality, and Gender," in *The House That Race Built: Black American, U.S. Terrain*, ed. Wahneema Lubiano (New York: Pantheon, 1997), 140.

24. Cheryl Clarke, "The Failure to Transform: Homophobia in the Black Community," in *Home Girls: A Black Feminist Anthology*, ed. Barbara Smith (New York: Kitchen Table/Women of Color Press, 1983), 200.

25. Williams, "Living at the Crossroads," 144.

26. Clarke, "Failure to Transform," 200.

27. Lorde, "Scratching the Surface," 51–52.

28. Nathan Hare and Julia Hare, *The Endangered Black Family: Coping with the Unisexualization and Coming Extinction of the Black Race* (San Francisco: Black Think Tank, 1984), 65.

29. Cheryl Sanders, "Christian Ethics and Theology in Womanist Perspective," in *Journal of Feminist Studies in Religion* 5, no. 2 (fall 1989): 90.

30. Jawanza Kunjufu, *Countering the Conspiracy to Destroy Black Boys* (Chicago: African American Images, 1985), 21.

31. Asante, *Afrocentricity*, 57.

32. Barbara Christian, *Black Feminist Criticism: Perspectives on Black Women Writers* (New York: Pergamon, 1985), 199.

33. Cheryl Clarke, "Lesbianism: An Act of Resistance," in *This Bridge Called My Back*, 131–32.

34. Ibid.

35. Barbara Smith, "Toward a Black Feminist Criticism," in *But Some of Us Are Brave*, ed. Gloria T. Hull, Patricia Bell Scott, and Barbara Smith (Old Westbury, N.Y.: Feminist Press, 1982), 171.

36. Patricia Hill Collins, *Black Feminist Thought: Knowledge, Consciousness, and the Politics of Empowerment* (Boston: Unwin Hyman, 1990), 194.

37. Ibid., 195.

38. Karen Baker-Fletcher and Garth Kasimu Baker-Fletcher, *My Sister, My Brother: Womanist and Xodus God-Talk* (Maryknoll, N.Y.: Orbis Books, 1997), 259.

39. Lorde, "Scratching the Surface," 49.

40. Smith and Smith, "Across the Kitchen Table," 124.

41. Clarke, "Failure to Transform," 197.

42. See Lorde, "Scratching the Surface," 48.

43. Boykin, *One More River*, 270–71.

44. Lorde, *Sister Outsider*, 110.

5: God-Talk and Black Sexuality

1. See Karl Barth, *The Humanity of God*, trans. J. N. Thomas and T. Wieser (Richmond: John Knox Press, 1960).

2. Carter Heyward, *Our Passion for Justice: Images of Power, Sexuality, and Liberation* (New York: Pilgrim Press, 1988), 184.

3. James B. Nelson, *Embodiment: An Approach to Sexuality and Christian Theology* (Minneapolis: Augsburg Publishing House, 1978), 18.

4. Heyward, *Our Passion for Justice*, 140.

5. Ibid., 141.

6. Audre Lorde, *Sister Outsider* (Freedom, Calif.: The Crossing Press, 1984), 55.

7. Patricia L. Hunter, "Women's Power–Women's Passion: And God Said, 'That's Good,'" in *A Troubling in My Soul: Womanist Perspectives on Evil and Suffering*, ed. Emilie M. Townes (Maryknoll, N.Y.: Orbis Books, 1993), 192.

8. Heyward, *Our Passion for Justice*, 21–22.

9. See Peter Paris, *The Spirituality of African Peoples: The Search for a Common Moral Discourse* (Minneapolis: Fortress Press, 1995).

10. Karen Baker-Fletcher and Garth Kasimu Baker-Fletcher, *My Sister, My Brother: Womanist and Xodus God-Talk* (Maryknoll, N.Y.: Orbis Books, 1997), 26.

11. Nelson, *Embodiment*, 18.

12. James A. Cone, *A Black Theology of Liberation*, rev. ed. (Maryknoll, N.Y.: Orbis Books, 1990), 94.

13. Ibid., 107.

14. Ibid., 108–9.

15. Delores S. Williams, "A Womanist Perspective on Sin," in *A Troubling in My Soul*, 144.

16. Ibid., 146.

17. Marjorie Hewitt Suchocki, "Sin," in *Dictionary of Feminist Theologies*, ed. Letty M. Russell and J. Shannon Clarkson (Louisville: Westminster/John Knox Press, 1996), 262.

18. Alice Walker, *In Search of Our Mothers' Gardens: Womanist Prose* (New York: Harcourt Brace Jovanovich, 1983), xi.

6: A Sexual Discourse of Resistance and the Black Church

1. Alice Walker, *The Color Purple* (New York: Washington Square Press/ Pocket Books, 1982), 177.

2. Audre Lorde, *Sister Outsider* (Freedom, Calif.: The Crossing Press, 1984), 59.

3. It should be noted that a second conference took place in July 1998 at Howard University School of Divinity. Some of the limitations of the first conference were addressed in the follow-up conference.

Index

abolitionist movement, 16

Africa: Christianity and, 121–22; early European contact with, 32–33; early stereotypes regarding women in, 36–37; homosexuality in, 98–99; and the sacredness of secular reality, 131–32; sexual mores and, 65, 66, 67

Afrocentrism, 98, 102

agape, 115

AIDS. See HIV/AIDS

Antichrist, the, 139

Aristotle, 28

Asante, Molefi Kete, 98, 102

athletes, 103

Atkins, John, 33

Augustine of Hippo, 26

Baker-Fletcher, Garth Kasimu, 5

Baker-Fletcher, Karen, 5, 105, 123

Baldwin, James, 13, 18–19, 135

Barry, Marion, 80

Barth, Karl, 113

Bartmann, Sarah, 33–35, 37, 148n.11

Beloved (Morrison), 76, 133–34, 137

Bibb, Henry, 66

Bible, the. See scripture

Black church, the: and enslaved Black women's sexual mores, 66; HIV/AIDS and, 2–3, 4; homosexuality and, 89–97; a sexual discourse of resistance and, 131–43; unwed mothers and, 83–84

blackness: the Bible and, 91; God and, 124; need for the Black community to celebrate, 75; nineteenth-century U.S. ideol-ogy about, 15–16; O. J. Simpson and, 57; White culture's denigration of, 18, 97, 123; White culture's fascination with, 24; White slaveholders' views of, 112

Black power movement, 82

Black sexuality: the Black church and, 2–3, 4–5, 139–41; elements of a discourse of resistance regarding, 68–72; in movies, 77–79; national religious summit on, 141–42; need for Black laywomen to address, 137–38; reasons for lack of discourse regarding, 67–68; slavery and, 33–35, 64–67; stereotypes of, 35–36, 45–59; ways to foster discourse on, 132–37; White culture and, 11–13, 14–16, 23–25, 33, 123–24; womanist theology and, 1–2, 129

Blassingame, John, 65

blues, the, 69–70

body, the: Foucault on, 22; God's love of the human, 123–24; the incarnation and, 118; White culture's deprecation of, 25–26

Boswell, John, 90

Boykin, Keith, 98–99, 106–7

Boyz in the Hood (film), 78

Bruce, Philip A., 46

Buchanan, Pat, 88

bucks: Black men viewed as, 45–50; the Simpson case and the stereotypes of Black, 57–58

Calvin, John, 26–27

castration, 47, 150n.4

Catholic church, Black, 4